Narcissism

Stop Suffering Abuse By Understanding Narcissistic Personality Disorder

(Escape From Self Centered Narcissistic Personalities And Emotionally Destructive Relationships)

Carol P Aniston

Published By **Simon Dough**

Carol P Aniston

Narcissism: Stop Suffering Abuse By Understanding Narcissistic Personality Disorder (Escape From Self Centered Narcissistic Personalities And Emotionally Destructive Relationships)

ISBN 978-1-77485-615-4

Legal & Disclaimer

The information contained in this ebook is not designed to replace or take the place of any form of medicine or professional medical advice. The information in this ebook has been provided for educational & entertainment purposes only.

The information contained in this book has been compiled from sources deemed reliable, and it is accurate to the best of the Author's knowledge; however, the Author cannot guarantee its accuracy and validity and cannot be held liable for any errors or omissions. Changes are periodically made to this book. You must consult your doctor or get professional medical advice before using any of the suggested remedies, techniques, or information in this book.

Upon using the information contained in this book, you agree to hold harmless the Author from and against any damages, costs, and expenses, including any legal fees potentially resulting from the application of any of the information provided by this guide. This disclaimer applies to any damages or injury caused by the use and application, whether directly or indirectly, of any advice or information presented, whether for breach of contract, tort, negligence, personal injury, criminal intent, or under any other cause of action.

You agree to accept all risks of using the information presented inside this book. You need to consult a professional medical practitioner in order to ensure you are both able and healthy enough to participate in this program.

Table of Contents

Chapter 1: Signs You Are In A Relationship With A Codependent Relationship

Everyone has their own inner tensions or wounds that bring the emotions which they do not wish to confront. Are you concerned that people could judge you based on your actions or what you're like? Are you concerned that you could be injured if you love someone , or end up being alone? These are the types of hurts which can trigger the development of a self-dependant nature. You may not realize the time or how this occurs. In this section, I'm going to present to you the symptoms of dependence. It is possible that you are not experiencing all of these symptoms but you might be suffering from some. However, it is essential to know if you're involved in a codependent relationship or not.

Internalized Shame

There are many emotions and thoughts that go with shame. Some of they include inadequacy, lack of worthiness and disconnection. There is a constant feeling that people can detect your weaknesses and you feel marginalized or outed. It's possible to hide in one corner and disappear. However, it's not always about your self-esteem since even those with good self-esteem face shame. Everybody experiences shame at one moment or another in their lives. If the guilt is preventing you from doing something you know is considered unacceptable to society and you feel shamed, it's an appropriate shame to feel like having a sexy urinal in public.

Shame can manifest in a variety of physical indicators and physical signs. One of them is withdrawing from any kind in eye contact perspiration or nausea, freezing, dizziness and many more. It is common to observe that once a person has experienced an embarrassing incident it is then a time when the shame disappears. In the situation of someone who is dependent the shame is triggered from the time they were children that this shame is kept in the mind. Even when the incident is long over but the guilt remains and is triggered periodically. It is as an open wound that does not heal. People feel ashamed of themselves, and this makes them feel less as an individual.

There will be an increase of normal shame, accompanied by persistent internalized shame. This type of shame can give an opportunity for anxiety and can last longer than other types of shame. It also triggers feeling of desperation and despair for the person who is codependent. Self-esteem is impacted as they begin to exhibit signs of codependency such as depressive, people-pleasing, addiction and more. An underlying sense of inadequacy is etched into the individual's mind at the point they begin taking on their own shame. They judge everything negatively and begin to compare them to others, particularly with the people they admire. It can cause jealousy and envy. If the jealousy motivates the person to set positive goals without causing any negative feelings towards the other person this is a good sign of jealousy. If you are uncomfortable that you've decided to take extreme actions, then it's awful.

Lower levels of self-esteem

Self-esteem differs from shame. It is about what you think of yourself, while the latter is just the feeling. This is where your personal view about yourself will be revealed. Based on what you feel about yourself, your self-esteem can be high or low. However, you must get one thing straight which is that self-esteem isn't a reflection of what others think about yourself, but rather the way you think about yourself. People who are dependent suffer from lower levels of self-esteem and therefore, they want approval from other people. They feel good or bad dependent on other things or even on others.

When you win in a competition , or you meet all deadlines, get a huge sense of happiness and joy. That's the feeling you get isn't it? It's exactly the same feeling people who have a good self-esteem feel throughout the day. However, for the majority of people, when they experience a setback, whether emotional or financial they are in a state of despair, but they are only feeling it for a short time and will not be around for a long time. It is important to remember that they are not a reflection of your self-esteem. External circumstances don't affect confidence in yourself. If people are confident in themselves they understand that the external environment is passing, and will never reflect on them as individuals. Thus, they do not be affected by the things.

However, in the case of those with poor self-esteem experience sadness and a sense of loss. They feel like they've lost everything they've ever had. This is especially the case for codependent individuals due to their self-esteem issues. They depend on external influences such as appearance, prestige and money or recognition from others to boost their self-worth. In reality nothing could influence your self-esteem if you don't let them. If your behavior is solely driven by the idea that you need the approval of others then you are not expressing self-esteem-based, even though you feel that you are a good person. It is because every feeling that you feel is dependent on what other people think about you.

Being a People-pleaser

One of the best indicators that you're a crowd to pleaser is when you are attempting to alter your entire behavior to be able to accept an individual. This type of behavior comes due to the fact that those who are codependents want other people to affirm their existence. They are unable to concentrate their lives around them. They are always looking for someone else to be able to see them as they do or even like them. If you're trying your best to please other people by becoming a crowd self-pleaser and you're in a relationship with a codependent partner.

People who are awed by others always seek approval from other people, and if there is a chance that they are not happy with someone they begin to feel stressed. They begin to give others priority over their own wants and needs and thoughts and opinions of other people become more important in their lives. They begin to shape their own self in any way they can in order to be the person they feel is acceptable to those around them. This is also observed in relationships. They strive to always be perfect and blend in, perform well, act like the one to be responsible or appear attractive. This can lead to humiliation, and they then begin covering up every injury.

You'll get more and isolated from your true self as you depend on external circumstances to gauge your mood. This can lead to the need to be connected to others or the desire to be a part of a group and seek approval. It's like how addicts react to a substance and then consumes it even though they know that the substance will cause nothing but harm. The drug will then feel the emptiness they feel in their lives.

Remember that pleasing people doesn't bring long-term benefits. It may provide you with short-term relief, but that's not the end of it. The more you depend on other people and the more dependent you become, the more addiction will escalate to the point where you're completely dependent on someone else. The problem with people-pleasing typically is first noticed in the early years of childhood. Children are often enticed by the belief that being able to satisfy all the wishes and needs of their parents can make them the perfect child or aid them to get through life.

They also believe that changing is the only way by that they will gain their parents' respect. They begin to associate their 'good' qualities to things that they think their parents would like. However parents generally have high expectations or strict rules, and may even discipline the child when he/she is not able to keep pace with their expectations. This affects the self-esteem the child, and causes them to be a crowd who is always pleasing.

People who please develop a belief system where they believe they're not loved in the way they appear. The same is true for codependents. They begin to become compliant because they believe it will earn their loved ones. They begin to reject all characteristics that they think aren't good enough for other people. They may even begin to eliminate personality traits because they're trying to be accepted by others.

Guilt

You may think that both shame and guilt are two identical items, but they're not. Shame is a feeling an individual has about themselves and that feeling is not good. In contrast, guilt is a feeling that stems from the things you've done or stated that falls below your standards , and could be in violation of the ethical principles you hold to. For codependents the guilt is felt and deeply buried in shame, and it is a heightened emotion that is difficult to rid. If you're feeling self-conscious, you could be thinking with, "I shouldn't have made that statement. However, as time passes you could even feel ashamed such as 'I'm unkind and selfish.'

Sometimes, guilt gets over time and accumulate into a level that is too much to bear. It could take away tranquility. It is important to recognize that you're human and by this, I am trying the fact that we also are feeling. However, for codependents, they have feelings that they feel ashamed of and are embarrassed about. They are judging their own emotions and are constantly wondering what should be expected of them. They feel guilty inside them when they're upset and constantly tell them that they shouldn't be having the feelings they are. When they're depressed they believe that something is wrong, however they aren't. They make a few perceived mistakes in their heads and from time to the time, they review the past actions and conversations and feel guilt for the alleged mistakes.

The numerous negative thoughts and emotions of codependency may affect your self-image. One common symptom that is seen in people who have recently had an breakup is that they constantly contemplate where they might have made a mistake. They'll try to adapt themselves to their spouse as best they can since they believe that allowing others to be more accommodating will make them feel more comfortable. They are afraid of what they want and don't assert themselves as they should. They are always judging themselves as indulgent, self-centered, and weak. They tend to believe that their needs are too burdensome and, therefore they can't ask for assistance from to help from others.

Another thing to be noticed among couples who codepend is the fact that they are irritated by what their partners feel. For instance, they may go to a cinema with their partner, but are left feeling guilty when their spouse doesn't enjoy the film. They aren't sure how to resolve the issue and keep their guilt in check. They avoid confronting their partner about the other person's behavior, and believe that it is them who should be accountable for what the other person did. They blamed themselves, even though they weren't at fault initially.

They feel so unworthy or unworthy, they are a target for punishment.

Sometimes, they even accept the unfair way that others treat them simply because they believe they deserve the brutal treatment.

Pursuing Perfectionism

There isn't anything called perfect in the world however, people want it with a fervor. It's just an illusion in the minds of other people. It's not something that is of reach. However, those who are inclined to be perfectionists aren't confident about what's beneficial for them. They believe that they're not good enough due to their inability to meet what they think is acceptable. They engage in a constant struggle with themselves and have an false self-esteem. This results in a constant cycle of self-judgment and self-shaming. All of this is not just related to one particular event in their lives but also to the entirety of their self.

Chapter 2: The What Are The Characteristics For Narcissistic Persuasion Disorder?

The grandiose self-importance of self-importance

A variety of traits have a connection with narcissism. However, grandiose seems to be the one that is the most notable. Narcissists are possessed of a bizarre perception of entitlement. In their minds, they're above all other people and are only looking to be regarded or a part of the most prestigious. They always seek praise and applause even though they've not done anything to merit any.

Their self-assuring sense of self-importance creates a belief that they are unique and can only be understood by a select group of people. When you speak to Narcissists about issues that relate to relationship and work they'll talk about how much they've contributed to the success of things and why they are blessed to be able to have these people in their life, and the fact that no one could be accomplished without their input and involvement. Narcissists think they're the ultimate one, the kings of jungle, and the main characters on the stage. In their pursuit to be recognized and regarded as the top individuals, places and things, narcissists often embellish or deny their achievements and skills The idea is for them to be regarded and considered to be the most outstanding in all circumstances.

A number of popular personalities across the world have been portrayed as having the traits of a narcissist. For instance, Kanye West is one performer who has frequently displayed the characteristics of narcissism. it has led some to believe that he suffers of Narcissistic personality disorder. One of the many instances that he displayed narcissistic tendencies was during an award ceremony and he came up onto the stage in the acceptance address of Taylor Swift and declare that she wasn't worthy of the award, and that somebody else was supposed to receive the award. He became the focal point and publicly insulted Taylor Swift, without considering her sentiments.

Narcissists believe that they have the ultimate authority, and everything they say must be taken as authoritative.

The Sense of Rights

When you interact with Narcissists, it is easy to discover that they are always seeking things done according to their own terms and that's because they believe because they believe that they're special. They are not interested in people who don't have anything to offer, nor are they willing to tolerate people who do not conform with their rules or meet their requirements.

Narcissists exhibit the "whatever I need is what I receive" attitude. Their perception of entitlement is so great that they think they are entitled to all good things and are believed to be the best even if they have no merit.

Narcissists constantly seek out the very best in people they meet, however they think that those individuals are not entitled to demand the same. In their eyes, concerned, their lives are a all-or-nothing and every person they interact with is bound by their standards and wishes. The most effective way to make the narcissists off is to break their wishes or demand something in exchange in exchange for a service you plan to do them.

Invariably, I want praise and admiration

Because narcissists have an ego that is overinflated that require constant fed, they are usually at the mercy of sycophants, who lavish them with praise constantly. If you study closely the personality of a narcissist, you'll see they have relationships that are unidirectional - they are always about how they will do for them, and not the opposite.

In the past, Adolf Hitler remains a iconic example of a world leader suffering from Narcissistic personality disorder. His unfounded and skewed beliefs of superiority led to the deaths of over six million Jews during the second World War. The devastation resulted from Hitler along with his selfish NAZI party members remains visible to this day as will the entire world. terrible events that took place during that 2nd World War in a quick manner.

Since narcissists constantly seek to boost their egos even if they aren't enough for them. this is why they view it as a act of betrayal when their worshipers behave in ways that are not in line with their expectations.

Living in a Bubble is a Supporter of Their Dreams

Because we live in a society that isn't tolerant of the mischief of everyday people Narcissists concoct fantasies that make them appear to be the most powerful. They re-create self-satisfying fantasies of beauty, power, and even success which keep them in total command and feel significant.

The irony of this scenario is that these fantasies serve to cover up the flaws in their own emptyness, shameful feelings and feelings of guilt.

People who suffer of Narcissistic personality disorder (NPD) typically appear strong, confident and confident when they are in public. They appear to be completely in control of any situation that they are in but they are easily shattered by other people or situations that blow their bubble.

One of the most effective ways to identify an narcissist is having an opposing view to theirs so that you can be able to witness their anger and defensiveness for yourself. Therefore, those who associate with narcissists must be sure to take care.

One person who was in a bubble was Jim Jones, a cult leader who orchestrated an mass murder of over 800 residents within Jonestown, Guyana, during the 1970s. In addition to other types of personality problems, Jones was known to display narcissistic traits throughout his life. one such example was his complete disregard for others' feelings. He justified the use of violence and sexual assault to help people to discover who they are as human. Jim Jones did a lot of harm to his followers because of his fantasies and his assertion of being God for his followers was a great way to spread his ideas and beliefs across his followers.

Jim has brainwashed his followers to such an extent that when he informed them that the world wasn't worth living they opted to live their lives in order to live the possibility of a better future.

Inflicts adversity on people without shame or guilt

Narcissists never think about the well-being of others in their decisions In other words they do not place themselves in others' shoes, or take into consideration the feelings of others while conducting their business.

Lack of understanding causes them think of people as objects to serve their goals. Narcissists are known to believe in things such as "the ends justify the means." Whatever they may try to influence people into believing they are concerned, their sly attitude is always clear for the public to see that they're just playing the game to further their goals.

A recent article on the internet that discussed the narcissistic characteristics of Madonna noted "She has always been one to stay away from the spotlight and try to put herself back in the spotlight. She's often criticized for being unreasonable with her employees, and has little sympathy for long hours or the working conditions of the employees she employs. In 2005, she was said that she had lobbied researchers and the government for the treatment of nuclear debris using the mysterious fluid known as kabbalah."

Incessantly bully, insult and intimidate others

While narcissists create enchanted kingdoms within their heads but their influence isn't restricted to their minds. They think they're the most successful at everything, and they have a problem when they meet people who possess skills they know they don't.

If narcissists meet people who are more well-known, sophisticated and well-known than they are they are frightened and use their primary form of defense which is disdain towards those who are more popular, advanced, and well-known. They are aware that they cannot measure with them, which is why they take an ego-trip, which includes hurling insults at others and insults, using demeaning language or even insults.

Respond to criticism with anger React to Criticism with Shame, Anger, and Humiliation

The people who suffer from Narcissistic personality disorders (NPD) have mastered how to make themselves believe that no one has it better than them. They are completely convinced of their method of living and are not willing to be criticized whether constructive or not.

Narcissists believe that they wear the most stylish outfits, owns the top car, is dating the most beautiful girl, and is able to comprehend maths better than anyone else. That's the belief system he/she is based on and any thought or criticisms are received with strong resistance, often in the form of anguish, or even embarrassment in reaction to criticism. The way they react to criticism is very inadequate and, even involved in relationships, they don't consider it a symbiotic relationship and instead view it as an ongoing competition in which you're either the top or bottom and either the winner or the losing.

If their actions or behavior are scrutinized instead of rethinking and admitting their mistakes They resort in fighting (e.g. hypersensitivity, denial, blame, temper tantrum, excuse-making, etc.) as well as other kinds that are passive aggressive.

Manipulation and Control

Narcissists make up one of the most manipulative groups of human beings that can be found on the the planet. Although they appear to take care of the people in their circle of friends, the truth is that they only attract to people who serve their own agendas. There are a number of instances where narcissists use their romantic partners, siblings or children, as well as friends and family members, etc. in order to conceal their weaknesses and shortcomings and they did not even know it.

They employ tactics such as blame, guilt blame as well as blame and guilt. In their attempt to deflect reality and make people feel less than themselves. That's how far they will go to control others and maintain their illusion of being the best and standing over everyone else.

Boundary Violations and Rule-Breaking

Because narcissists have the status of kings and queens in their mind They do not feel that they are bound to adhere to the same rules as other people follow. While it could be different from person to person however, it's normal for narcissists not to attend the schedule and arrive whenever they want, ignore the promises they make to others and disobey traffic laws and even take items out and not return them, etc.

Narcissists are deluded to the point that they think of people as extensions of themselves. This is a grave problem as they don't respect others spaces and overtimes. which can lead to sexual violence, violent abuse and domestic violence, hate crimes and even the death of a loved one.

Projection of False Image

Narcissists aren't just recognized as pathologically deceiving They are also notoriously deceivers. They present false representations of themselves to all they meet which is why many people have been victims to these types of people.

In all their interactions, they present themselves as the absolute most prestigious of their kind socially, politically academically, financially romantically, sexually and professionally, etc. Their main motivation is self-aggrandizement and at the same time they do not look up or make fun of others.

When you are not close and personal with Narcissists, it's extremely difficult to determine the real person behind them and what they're doing, as their exterior appearance and manner of speaking are deceiving and manipulative to put it mildly. They make up a spectacle for their unsuspecting victims, but reveal their true colors once people become comfortable with them.

The concept behind this false perception is that it will make people to feel comfortable so that they can easily manipulate them and make use of them to satisfy their needs and desires. When they come across people who are unable to comprehend their selfish and sadistic motives, they face problematic, since they realize they are unable to control their opponents and, as such, respond with insults and talk about them.

It is the goal for every narcissist revered and appreciated for their supposed greatness. They are convinced of being exceptional and therefore are worthy of love, respect and respect from everyone other.

Invalidation of the Emotional Coercion System and invalidation

The effects of emotional coercion and character insufficiency are two of the most harmful characteristics of narcissists. This is especially true on those who are around their daily. If you interact with children, spouses and close friends, or even employees of narcissists you'll find that at times their self-confidence is weak and they lack a sense of decisiveness. this is because of years of coercion by emotion and character insufficiency.

Narcissists ensure that their loved ones and their friends are placed under them at all times. those who do not agree with these motives are branded and viewed as enemies, while those who are a part of the game are transformed into praise singers.

In their efforts to cause people to be unhappy and to keep them out of balance Narcissists spread negativity everywhere they go. They dismiss the feelings, emotions and opinions. They aren't concerned about the hurt they cause to other people's lives. Their self-centered mentality causes them to blame others for all the things that go wrong. It's not appropriate to hear an egotist say things like "I wouldn't have been so angry in the event that you weren't so dumb," or "we would have won the contract had you let me make the proposal and let me present it myself."

In most cases Narcissists don't pose any physical danger (such as physical assault or harassment or rape, or threats to their lives) However they have capabilities that can harm people emotionally and mentally.

Perfectionism

We live in a time in which perfection is not possible and that's why that we must always try to be the best we can every single day. Being the most excellent you can be and aiming for to be the best is a great characteristic, however, people who are narcissists be obsessed with the need for things to be always perfect. They set unreasonable expectations for themselves and the people around them. Then when these expectations do not meet then they start throwing angry and unhappy - it's no wonder they're always complaining. If you have an egocentric boss you'll find that it's difficult to please him or her The demands are constantly increasing and the lack of appreciation is depressing.

The lack of leadership and accountability

Narcissistic individuals always try to control their lives; However, their smugness prevents them from taking on responsibility unless things go according to plan. When problems arise and they don't have a solution to real problems and blame everybody else, not even them.

Since they live in a constant belief in their own perfection and self-esteem, they constantly blame everything other than themselves for their mistakes whether it's the judge, police officer or friend, colleague or even a sibling. Whatever the situation the issue must be the fault of someone else.

In all of this those that are suffering the most are those who have a strong emotional attachment to them.

They are constantly splitting actions and Reactions

There aren't any grey areas for narcissists. It's either white or black, which is a good indicator of their thinking process. They separate all things into two distinct parts: bad and good; when positive events occur they take full accountability and are praised while the moment things don't go as planned they assign blame to other people.

Narcissists can't mix memories of good and bad and prefer to split them into good and bad. For instance, Chris was blamed for more than 30 years of guilt because the time he was away from home while his wife was pregnant with their first child. the reason was because Chris was stuck on the streets of New York during a snowstorm. Jenny described the entire vacation as to be a complete disaster and one of the worst she's ever had because the weather was not sunny and her hotel was not as nice as she imagined it was going to be.

Incapable of communicating and working as a part of a Team

In order for any relationships (social as well as professional) to be successful everyone involved must try to learn about the strengths, weaknesses and emotions.

Before you take action in any way, you'll have to ask yourself questions such as: If I did this what will the person feel? Do we feel happy? What will the impact be on our relationship? Why should I not or should I?

These are legitimate questions to be addressed and considered as it is through interactions such as these that real relationships are formed. Narcissists, unfortunately, are not capable of these thoughts, and they don't possess the drive to think about trying.

Narcissists don't understand the feelings of others They aren't willing to compromise and don't even care.

Chapter 3: What Are The Signs Of A Covert Narcissist

Being around a narcissist who is covert is a daunting experience and this is why it's important to recognize the character traits that dominate their lives. In reality, there do not have any physical body tests one could perform to identify the existence of the narcissist. It is however possible to be able to observe certain behaviours and reactions , and determine if it is a problem. This list contains 12 points derived from the standard guide offered in the Diagnostic Manual of Mental Illness Fifth Edition (DSM5) as well as other crucial observations from different experts in this area.

A inflated sense of self-importance

Psychologists refer to this trait as grandiose. It is the hallmark trait for narcissism , and it goes far beyond vanity or arrogance.

The world is filled with narcissists there exists a clear hierarchy that places them at the highest level. They must be the best capable, most knowledgeable possess everything and control everyone. Also everything must be done according to their rules as this will be the sole way to feel secure.

They believe they are unique and exceptional and only want to be in contact with other "unique." In the same way they are far too great for everything ordinary or common and will only be able to connect with the highest-ranking individuals and things

Narcissists believe they are more superior than everyone other people and they will never want to be recognized even when they clearly do not merit the recognition they deserve. They exaggerate their accomplishments and skills and make everyone feel privileged to be surrounded by them. They are the most revered heroes and all others are at the bottom of their list.

A sense of entitlement and Prestige

Because of their over-inflated value Narcissists are conditioned to receive a favorable treatment everywhere they go. They feel unique and believe they are entitled to everything they desire. They want everyone around them to be available at their call and to fulfill their every whim and wish. If you do not comply and satisfy their every requirement They will dismiss them as unimportant.

A naive need for praise and Admiration

The vanity of Narcissists is like a balloon which requires a continuous flow with air in order to remain inflating. In the same way, their egos require constant praise and affirmation to keep it inflating. Every now and then, a compliment doesn't make a difference, which is the reason why people surround themselves those who will nourish their egos with affirmations and praise.

The interactions are unidirectional as it's constantly about how the person who is in love is able to do to the narcissist , and not vice versa. And in the event of any breach or reduction of appreciation or praise from the person who is being admired and the narcissist views it as disloyalty and the person who is devoted will suffer severe consequences.

The most striking aspect of the issue is that regardless of the level of praise or approval that the narcissists are given but they do not feel they are good enough. They do not feel self-assured, and regardless of their grandiose and arrogance, they're extremely nervous and insecure. They believe that no one will ever truly love them, and hide this by continually seeking applause and praise from other people. Their insatiable desire for compliments and praise is typically an attempt to boost their fragile self-esteem.

Living In A Utopian World Which Supports Their Illusions

Because the reality of reality doesn't support their fantasies of grandeur, Narcissists live in a realm of fantasy. They live in a dream world that is created by their mystical thinking of self-deception, distortion, and distortion. The false perceptions are defined by fantasies of unending beauty, success power, brilliance and ultimately, a perfect world. The false thoughts that are fabricated can make people feel like they are like they are special and in control, obscuring their real feelings of shame and emptyness.

Narcissists are prone to dwell in this imaginary bubble and anything that could threaten to blow it up is met by a heightened defensiveness and range. The facts and opinions that frighten their minds are brushed aside or rationalized. Therefore, those around the narcissist need to be aware of their movements in order to ensure peace. They have a misguided perception of the world that surround them.

Inability To Empathize With Others

Narcissists cannot feel the emotions of others. That is, they are unable to place themselves in others' position, but they can exploit others without shame or guilt. For them, those around them are there to meet their needs and satisfy their unending desire for acceptance.

To achieve this they aren't hesitant about using others to fulfill their goals. Most of the time the exploitation is obvious however in some cases it's invisible and is difficult to spot.

Narcissisms do not think about the impact their manipulative behavior has on others. Even when you attempt to point it out their actions, they don't understand. They are only concerned with the way to satisfy their own needs and satisfy their egos.

Narcissists are also known to belittle, denigrate and intimidate others. This is apparent when they meet somebody who seems to have something that they do not have. A person who's more well-known more confident, or someone who doesn't surrender to their wishes and desires. Narcissists combat this by creating a feeling of disdain for those who are like them. It's their way of defending themselves. The only way to boost their self-esteem is to bring an individual down by showing that they don't care at all and how much they value the person around them.

Carefulness

Narcissists often have a excessive perception of perfection. They believe that things must be exactly as they planned, and that life should go the way they imagine it in their mind. This is a nonsensical expectation in reality which leaves the narcissist being down and miserable constantly.

Narcissists who seek perfection can be very difficult to satisfy. Everything you do won't be sufficient, and you must always satisfy their endless demands for love, admiration and service or purchase. If you fail to fulfill these requirements, it can result in your being dismissed. They are not able to say "no" and frequently anticipate others to disrupt themselves to serve them.

They'd like to be in Control

We've discovered that many people who are narcissists strive for perfection. when they find that things aren't going according to their standards they begin to develop this overwhelming desire to control other phrases. They will do everything to take control of the situation and then manipulate it in their own way.

With their unreasonable feeling of entitlement, they'll try to be in control of events since they believe it's the right thing to do. They have everything planned out in their heads. They have a plot in their mind and have assigned distinct roles to everyone within the particular setting. If any one of them behaves differently to the script, the narcissist gets angry because they have not understood the details of the script. You pose a threat to their intended outcome. What they consider you to be is nothing more than a character in their inner play, not an actual human being with his own thoughts and feelings.

Participate In The Blame Game

Although the narcissist may want to control the situation but they do not want to be held accountable for a negative outcome. If things don't go according to their goals or plans The narcissist puts the blame and responsibility on someone else. The problem is not theirs and not someone else's. The narcissist may also assign blame to everyone else: all teachers are equal as all police officers are corrupt and so on. All they can do is attribute the blame on a specific person or system, like parents, siblings, the laws of the land, etc.

Most of the time the narcissist will blame the person who is closest and most emotionally connected to them. This person with a strong and loyal admirer is the one to blame since the odds of deflecting or absconding with the responsibility are slim. The person who is narcissistic must maintain the illusion of perfection and this is only done by continuously assigning blame to somebody or something else.

Thrill-Seekers

Narcissists are addicts to adrenaline who stray from their inseparable desire to be loved and be awed by others. They'll discuss the overwhelming circumstance in depth, or try to get the attention of people in their vicinity. If you try to confront them about the risks they're exposing themselves to through being adrenaline addicts, they will promptly dismiss you. They will try to tell that everyone around them isn't worth their time, and that's why they are involved in risky activities to make a difference.

Anyone who works with a narcissist is likely to encounter the middle of a rollercoaster, moving around in various directions. You'll follow what brings most enjoyment to the person who is narcissistic. If the adrenaline rush is on the brain, plans for strategic thinking are tossed out the window and replaced with the self-inflicted stress. The fact is that a an addict is always seeking adrenaline as the resultant enthusiasm makes them feel better about themselves. The thrill also serves as a means of releasing all the stress and anger that are usually bottled up inside them.

Extreme Sensitivity to Criticism

Narcissists believe that they have to be viewed as flawless superior or infallible. You can be either perfect or insignificant. They believe that the middle ground doesn't exist. They will not tolerate the slightest kind of criticism since they are living in a realm that is a fantasy world where no crime are committed. So, no matter what you say strategies they could use to modify their behaviour, they'll be defensive or completely withdrawn. They'll say anything in an attempt to justify their behavior and they'll want you to accept their reasoning and go forward with their lives as usual.

They'll attack and throw every kind of insult to their opponents and then remove them from their apparent enthralling presence. Narcissists expect their adversaries to be in shock when they do they are not on their radar and it makes them feel confidence and worthiness.

Surprisingly, those who are afraid to be criticised are frequently critical of others. They recognize their own shortcomings, however, they believe that others have issues and require be changed.

Inability To Sense Humor

Narcissists are way too serious to live. They aren't able to appreciate jokes and don't even create jokes, aside from some sarcastic comments and strange puns. The lack of understanding causes them incapable of understanding the emotional and contextual aspects of the actions, words or jokes displayed. To be able to be able to laugh at a joke or to make it a funny and relevant one, he or she must first , comprehend the context and impact of those around him. Narcissists aren't aware of this and therefore are prone to sarcasm. They mistake it as intelligence.

There is no defined boundary between personal and professional.

Narcissists see others as an extension of themselves. They don't know the point at which they've reached and where another person starts. They see the other person as merely to serve themselves and will ignore their family, needs, obligations, or other obligations which their loyal followers need to perform. They are thought of as 'narcissists on supply', who are primarily to satisfy their own individual needs. As such, it's hard for a narcissist to imagine them as a decent person. They usually expect their followers are at to their.

The blurred boundaries can cause people to in a way that they dominate conversations, and even divulge intimate details of their lives. They're likely to talk about embarrassing events they've done or shared without thinking about what others will think of the statements. They are likely to boast about their accomplishments or use phrases that others might consider offensive, insulting and in general offensive.

Chapter 4: A Self-Importance

Prestige is an over the high feeling of popularity that is not simply an aspiration or pride. Narcissists believe that they're exceptional and "extra" and believe that other remarkable people are able to observe them. In reality, they're extremely suitable for things that are standard or normal. They should be connected to and be associated with other people places, things, and spots that are of a high-end status.

Narcissists always believe they are more superior than other person and deserve praise in the same way, regardless of whether they've ever actually been able to. It is common for them to make up their achievements and talents or to lie both inside and outside. When they're discussing fellowships or jobs they'll only talk about the number of people they're working with and how successful they are as well as how blessed they are being surrounded by people. They're the pioneers and each one of them is the minor players at best.

lives in a world of fantasy that enhances their dreams of awe

Because reality isn't helping their distorted view of them, narcissists reside in a realm of fantasies supported by self-double dealing and inexplicably cryptic reasoning. Self-exalting figments make us feel attractive and responsible for their endless success, vitality, ingenuity as well as a flawless love. These daydreams protect us from the feelings of self-pity and blame , while at the same time absolving the facts and conclusions that are in contradiction to their beliefs. Anything that attempts to blow out the air pockets of daydream is met with a sense of extreme protection and even anger, and those who surround the narcissist must take their disbelief of reality with care.

The need for constant praise and reverence

The narcissist's sense of omnipotence appears like a balloon which gradually disappears without a sufficient flow of praise and affirmation to ensure it is expanded. Sometimes it's not enough. Narcissists require constant food for their self. They are constantly surrounded by people who are eager to fulfill their highest expectations to be confirmed. They are not asymmetrical interactions. It's about what the person who is admiring can achieve for the narcissist and not vice versa. Furthermore that if the confidence of the admirer is ever compromised or reduced and the narcissist considers that to be a loss.

A feeling of being qualified

Narcissists want the best treatment because it is their right due to their belief in themselves as extraordinary. They believe that they must achieve anything they want. They also expect those who surround them to fulfill their every need and urge programed. This is the primary expectation of them. If you're not expecting and meeting their requirements then you're ineffective. Furthermore in the event that you are able to compromise your principles or ask for something "egotistically" to get it be prepared to defend yourself against a savage anger, resentment or a cold shoulder.

Inflicts harm on others, without shame or blame

Narcissists do not develop the capacity to recognize the feelings of others and to place themselves in the position of other people. So, empathy is not enough. People view people as objects in a variety of ways, there to fulfill their needs. They don't even think about using others to reach their goals. This kind of abuse can be occasionally a cause for concern but it's usually ignored. Narcissists aren't aware of how others influence their behaviour. In addition in the event you do find out, they're unlikely to admit the message. What they are most familiar with is the requirements for their particular needs.

Ofttimes, it is possible to disparage threats, menaces or disparages others

Narcissists can be harmed whenever they encounter someone who appears to be in possession of something they want particularly those who are successful and well-known. Anyone who doesn't bow to them or contest them in any manner also risk compromising their own integrity. They are criticized for their security aspect. The most effective method of eliminating the danger and elevating their self-esteem is to eliminate these men. You can do it in a patronizing manner or in a manner that is smug to show how insignificant the other person is planning to show them. On the other hand, using slurs, harassment or provoking people, they may go on edge in order to force the other person back to conform.

Do not give in to the fantasy

Narcissists are often charming and attractive. We're skilled in creating an amazing mental perception that attracts us. Their evident trust and big desires draw us in. The more shaky our faith and the less we trust, the more captivating is the attraction. It's not difficult to become entangled in your web of illusions, thinking that they'll fulfill our desire to feel more powerful and alive. However this is just an idea, and that is one that is expensive.

Your requirements won't be met (or even recognized).

It is important to note that narcissists don't seeking accomplices is crucial

They are looking for admirers who are loyal to them. The only thing a narcissist has is in being able to demonstrate to them that they are incredibly special to enhance their self-satisfying image. It doesn't record your thoughts and thoughts.

Check out the way that the narcissist behaves towards others.

Being a manipulative, lying, damaging people, and shaming them In all likelihood treat you in a the same way. Do not fall for the idea that you're special and will be protected.

Get rid of the rose-colored glasses.

It's important to look at the people you choose to associate with as they are as a significant part to your existence, and not as who you want to make them. Stop apologizing for bad behavior or reducing the harm caused by it. Refusing to acknowledge it won't make it disappear. Narcissists are extremely resistant to change, and the primary question you should to ask yourself is on the chance that you will live to the eternal you.

Make yourself a focus upon your personal fantasies.

Concentrate on what you want for yourself instead of becoming lost in the fantasies of the self-centered narcissist. What are the things in your life that you would like to alter? What kind of legacy do you wish to establish? In order to make your dreams a realisation, what goals do you need to give up?

Set firm boundaries

Solid relationships depend on respect and respect for each other. In any event they are connected they are unable to conduct genuine correspondence. It's not because they think that they'd like to not; they simply aren't. They can't see you. They don't hear what you say. We don't see them as a person who doesn't fit in with their desires. Therefore, narcissists occasionally and then push others' boundaries. With an eloquent sense of privilege they behave in this way.

Narcissists do not think about experiencing or getting your possessions with out your consent.

They may be sneaking through your private messages and mail as well as listening in on phone calls, and yelling in without greeting, ignoring your thoughts into consideration, and giving your unwelcome assessments and advice. They could even let you know things they think or feel about you. Understanding what they are is crucial and you can start setting more beneficial limits to ensure that your requirements are met.

Create an arrangement.

If you've had a tendency for a long time for encouraging others to ignore your boundaries, taking back control isn't easy. Make sure you are aware of your goals and possible issues to position yourself for success. What are the major changes you're planning to implement? Have you ever been in contact with a narcissist who worked before? Any other information you're not sure of? What is the proportion of power in your group, and how is the arrangement going to impact your situation? What is the best way to approve the new outskirts? This will aid you in the evaluation of your choices and create an effective plan to respond to these questions.

Think about a delicate methodology.

If you need to maintain your relationship with your narcissist you'll have to take your time. You're hurting their self-image of perfectness by drawing the attention of their violent or unfaithful behavior. Find them graciously, skillfully and as compassionately as you can to convey the message. Be aware of how their actions and actions, in contrast to their thoughts and objectives, cause the person to experience. Be quiet while they react with anger and a sense of security. If it is possible you are able to disappear, then continue the conversation.

Do not draw a line unless you're willing to hold it.

You can trust the narcissist to challenge boundaries and check your cutoffs Be prepared. Keep track of the suggestions made. You've sent a message to the company that in the event that you decide to return not to be taken seriously.

Set up to accommodate any interactions that may arise.

The effort you make to take the responsibility for your life can make the narcissist to feel weakened and irrational. They're used to being described as. To get redress in different areas of the relationship they may increase their demands, eject themselves from you, or try to control or convince you to give up the new boundaries. It's up to your ability to remain solid.

Do not think about things in terms of literality

To ask to be shielded from the resentments of inadequacy or blame, narcissists must constantly ignore their flaws or grotesqueness, as well as missteps. You'll often be doing this by pointing out their flaws to others. To be blamed for things that aren't your fault or being portrayed as having attributes you don't have is extremely upsetting. Try not to accept it for what it can be however it happens. It's not all about you.

Do not accept the narcissist's interpretation of you are.

In reality, narcissists do not live in the present, which is evident from their views on other people. Do not allow your self-confidence to sabotage your humiliation and your habitual pettiness. Avoid acknowledging outlandish risk and/or fault or to make an the results of your analysis. The narcissist has to maintain the pessimism.

Avoid interacting with the narcissist.

The purpose of being questioned is to defend your own position and counter the Narcissist. However you're likely to not get them to be able to understand you regardless of how objective you appear or how convincing your argument is. Thus, protecting your argument may be a problem in the situation. Be careful not to waste your time. Tell the narcissist you're not able to help but contradict their assertion, and then proceed.

Be aware of yourself.

A good sense of self is the most effective defense against the dangers of a narcissist's and predictions. It is easier to overlook any off-the-wall analysis made against you when you are aware of your strengths and weaknesses.

Release the requirement to endorse.

It is crucial to disengage yourself from the viewpoint of the narcissist as well as the desire to please or please them to your own satisfaction. They must know the truth independently regardless of whether the narcissist has an alternative viewpoint on the situation.

Seek help and find a the reason is somewhere else

If you're likely to stay in a marriage that is manipulative be realistic about what you should and shouldn't anticipate from yourself. A narcissist will never transform into someone who admires yourself, which is why you'll have to seek out help and personal satisfaction elsewhere.

Find out what solid relationships closely are like.

When you are a member of an egocentric family, you may not have a good idea of what a solid blessing-and-take relationship looks like. If you follow the dictator model of shakiness you'll feel comfortable. Just be aware that as pleasant as it may sound but it can make you be uncomfortable. You'll feel respected as well as awed by, and relaxed to be in relationship with each other.

Spend time with those who will give you an accurate impression of who you are. is.

To be able to adjust and refrain from being entangled in the falsehoods of the narcissist spending time with those who are aware of who you really are and applauding your thoughts and feelings is essential.

Find new friends If necessary, outside the circle of narcissists.

In order to more easily be in control, a few people who are narcissists cut off the people in their lives. If you're in this scenario you must invest some effort into the rebuilding or developing new relationships.

Seek meaning and purpose when it comes to volunteering, work and other activities.

Instead of focusing on the narcissist who makes you to feel better and proud, try finding challenging exercises which make the most of your talents and let you contribute.

How do you leave a Narcissist?

It's difficult to break up a bitter connection. It is particularly difficult to cut ties with a narcissist as they are so captivating and captivating, regardless of the beginning of the relationship, or when you're taking steps to end the relationship. It is easy to be awestruck by the manipulative behaviour of the narcissist. You may be into a state of mind that you are unable of endorsements or perhaps you feel "gaslighted" and doubt your own judgment. If you're both dependent and dependent, your need to be unwavering, which can be more than the necessity to safeguard your confidence and self-confidence. But, it is important to remember that in a marriage, no one is entitled to be victimized, intimidated or neglected internally and verbally. There are ways to separate yourself from the narcissist and also the shame and self-fault and proceed in the process of healing.

You can learn about the narcissistic personality problem.

The more you study the more you learn about the methods that can be employed by a narcissist to keep you into the relationship. A narcissist is known to frequently resurrect the love and adulation ("love blasting") after you decide to go away, which caused you to join the initial. They may also provide incredibly strong assurances that they do not have a goal to alter their behaviour.

Write down the reasons for your going to leave.

Be clear about what the reason for the relationship to be ended will prevent you from getting enticed back. Keep your list handy via the internet, or on your phone device, and refer back to it when you start to ask yourself questions or the narcissist is able to turn on the charm or presents astonishing arguments.

Look for help.

The narcissist could have damaged your relationships with family members or stifled your activities in public throughout the time you were together. There's no one else like you regardless of what you like, no matter what your circumstances. Furthermore in the event that you're unable to meet up with old acquaintances You can seek help by contacting help gatherings, emergency lines as well as asylums for people who have a violent habit in the home.

Do not try to erase the dangers.

It's better to accept that the narcissist will not change and will only leave once you've set the rules. Proclamations or threats can only alarm the narcissist, making it difficult to be free.

After you've left

It might be a huge blow to their sense of authority and ego to abandon the narcissist. The truth is that we must be mindful of their massive self-image, which is why they'll continue trying to take control of your behavior. If they find that engaging and "love to shell" does not work it is possible to use threats by slandering you in front of friends and colleagues or following you on online networking sites or face-to-face.

Do not contact any narcissists.

The more time you spend in contact to them the greater confidence you can provide them with the assurance that they won't be able to lure you back into. It is easier to keep the distance and stay away from their online live messages, messages and messages. If you share children include other people for every arranged change in the care of your children.

Let yourself be alone and lament.

The separation of a couple, no matter what the reason are often very painful. Any time you cut off a toxic relationship could cause you to feel pathetic as well as angry, confused and grieve over losing shared goals and obligations. Regaining the connection will require an expenditure, making it anything less than difficult to be by yourself and rely on family members.

Don't try that you can convey your sorrow to the person who is a narcissist.

When the message is absorbed that you can no longer maintain your self-esteem The narcissist is likely to continue to harm an individual within the moment. They won't suffer any resentment or guilt and will only have that constant need to be praised and acknowledged. This isn't an assessment of the person you are, but rather an indication of their relationships being always uneven.

Due to the very nature of the condition, the majority of people suffering from NPD aren't willing to admit that they are suffering from the condition, and considerably less likely to ask for assistance. Whatever the case in fact, it's difficult to tackle a an issue of narcissism in the character. But this doesn't mean there's no expectation or that it's unreasonable to anticipate adjustments. In extreme situations states of mind stabilizers, antidepressants and prescriptions for antipsychotics are currently being directed or when the NPD is associated with another illness. Psychotherapy, be that it may, is an most important treatment method of the time.

You can determine the best way to take responsibility for your actions through a conversation with an expert therapist. create a greater sense of the extent of your actions, and establish better connections. Your enthusiasm (EQ) is also able to be developed. The ability to comprehend, utilize your feelings in a manner that is able to empathize with others, effectively share an understanding, and establish strong connections. It is also possible at any time to become familiar with the skills that comprise an enthralling knowledge.

Chapter 5: How Do Be A Narcissist Feel Jealous?

Before figuring out the best way to make an narcissist feel jealous, it's crucial to be aware of the dangers it could be if done in the wrong manner. Jealousy is among the emotions that could be a major influence on the thoughts, choices and movements. Narcissistic criminals who scored higher on psychopathy committed their crimes due to jealousy. A positive psychopath-narcissist became requested why he devoted homicide, and he stated that a man he killed was riding a high-priced automobile than his. This suggests that some jealousy can cause a narcissist to act to take a risk if they are sick enough.

There is a good chance that less people who are narcissists have psychopathic tendencies and the majority of them will never make it through the line of homicide. But that doesn't mean that it's completely secure to make them be jealous. If they're provoked enough it is possible for them to cause emotional harm to you or cause any other type of covert damage.

A method to make use of the power of jealousy to the Narcissist

It is possible to cause a narcissist to be jealous by attempting to impress them or harm their feelings to cause them to feel the bitter taste of being hurt. I'll go over each scenario in this piece in detail since they require unique strategies.

Before proceeding similar manner, it is essential to remember that you're in the narcissist's realm. They are playing their most favorite game, and they're more experienced. Narcissists are highly manipulative and jealousy is many of their most effective tools to control other people, particularly when it comes to relationships. Even parents with narcissistic tendencies make use of jealousy in the form of preferring a select group of children over other kids in the hope of controlling their children without difficulty.

To ensure that you're by no way out of the loop, you might need to be more clever than them, and employ methods that they don't know about.

How to make use of Jealousy in order to draw an Narcissist

If you're the narcissists and wish to convince them that you feel the same, jealousy is one of the emotions that can trigger enchantment that is not only for narcissists however anyone. The type of jealousy that works in this instance is when they are jealous of another because they are in love with you.

How do I do it?

Begin by offering the narcissist a fascination if you've been unable to keep it. If they begin to feel the narcissist's behavior, stop and begin showing a passion in someone else. I'm not saying that you should convince someone to start admiring you to make them look like an person who is a narcissist. Simply approach the man you want to be with in a manner that is friendly while not ignoring the narcissist. it will be enough to make them jealous.

This is an important aspect to remember. Narcissists perceive human beings as the black and white of their world, either worthy or unworthy. The way in which they consider worth can enhance the art work as it may challenge their individual superiority. The goal is to get people to inquire " have I changed into this person preferred because that he's superior to me?" If this comes to their minds then they could take every step to prove that they're superior than their counterpart.

Be aware that narcissists are aware of this game more. If you conduct yourself with a clear intention it will be noticed quickly, and it may cause harm. You must conceal your intentions as much amount as you can when you're trying to impress an individual's attention.

It is important to mention that you're supposed to most effectively employ jealousy when you are trying to impress an narcissist, and not when you are relationship. The book I wrote "the last guidebook to make an alliance with a narcissist a success," I defined how jealousy can harm a relationship.

Discipline a Narcissist with Jealousy

The most effective way to create jealousy that could cause harm to a narcissist is to appear to be successful and happy than they already are. However, accomplishing this in the hopes of hurting them the most isn't as easy and it's not worth the effort. Instead, it's better to consider the option to get revenge first. This is typically due to the fact that they haven't yet moved from the past completely. In my essay "why do narcissists change their ways so quickly "I said that the need to get revenge is a strong indicator that a person isn't yet completely over the hump.

The Narcissist in you desires to make you Feel awestruck

A number of typical behaviours that are seen in people with Narcissism are actions that can harm their relationships, and specifically is a sign that they are looking for romantic partners. They'll be flirting openly or more calculatingly even though they're pretending not to notice the fact that they're in your presence or spend their time talking about how attractive they think others are to them from the other end of the spectrum of traits, specifically those you don't show.

In the past, it was unclear why people who are narcissists could, in the end, in the long run, stop eating as they are constantly looking for praise and encouragement that everyone is looking for of their company. The absence of a large others through their personal conduct could seem counterintuitive and could cause problems regarding their self-esteem.

This is something that the majority of trust narcissists have to deal with to an equal basis, regardless of appearing confident in their abilities and

charm. It's been suggested that these behavior patterns could be employed deliberately by the narcissists in order to make their friends feel
betrayed. Many narcissists' courting actions include acting unattached or unengaged, looking for attractive potential partners or flirting, chatting about attractive alternatives with you, etc. Are there any behaviors that are commonly used to cause jealousy within a romantic relationship?

Where Did Narcissism Where Does Narcissism Come From?

In the same way it is true that there are certain more complex theories of narcissism and narcissism, the most basic guidance is that it results from a struggle between two different notions of self-worth. On one side, there are instilled feelings of inferiority. On the other side, there are surface feelings of superiority that keep the narcissist in ignorance of their own feeling of inadequateness. The possibility of masking feeling of inadequacy by the perception of superiority requires constant reinforcement from other people.

Narcissism is believed by some to disguise a source of self-doubt as well as an inability to feel self-worth. One method of analyzing where the narcissism is rooted is to see it as a means of coping. When their self-deflection is suppressed, they are unable to normally manipulate it to subvert the issue completely. It can become overwhelming when it comes to the surface.

This is a major reason due to the fact that they aren't equipped with coping strategies for dealing with the situation. An effective method to hide their negative self-image is to hide it from the evens them is to expand their narcissistic characteristics with the aim of altering their self-image. They also try to change what they believe to be the other person's perceptions of themselves.

Their method of altering their self-perceptions isn't optimal or adaptive. One of the most common strategies they employ is jealousy. They do this according to what they believe inside, which will make them being jealous. It could cause you to be unhappy, but in the minds of the narcissists they have received the conflict.

Narcissists often engage in actions that cause anyone to feel uneasy and jealous. When you begin to feel unhappy, they could claim that you are overreacting and the fact that this is proof of all the issues that you've had.

Much of this kind of behavior happens when the person who is narcissist feels jealous of something that is associated with their love interest. Their responses are tactical in that a number of narcissist's relationship-threatening behavior is strategic to re-setup the status quo.

Retribution and dominance motives are typical responses for narcissists when they are confronted or their self-confidence is at risk. If they feel that they are being viewed as jealous, their first reaction is to seek to gain control over the situation to gain the situation. They attempt to exact revenge by revealing to their accomplice that they'll never be treated that way even though their jealousy is usually unfounded.

The third and final motives are to boost their low self-image. They want to determine if they're surrounded by someone who truly is interested in them, seeking relationship security and compensating for low self-esteem.

If you're partner with someone who is highly narcissistic and are planning to stay in the relationship, but the individual seems to attempt to make you jealous continuously There are a few things you could consider doing. Start by determining the motives behind the behavior. This might give you clues as to the possibility that they are trying to fuel your jealousy solely because they're insecure, or whether or not they're compensatory actions. Once you've got this knowledge, you'll be able to deal with the situation when your partner attempts to cause jealousy due to their own anxieties.

How can we distinguish between codependency from Narcissism?

Narcissists (a person suffering from Narcissistic personality disorder) or codependents generally thought of as opposites, however even though their behavior might differ but they do share a lot of psychological traits. In reality, narcissists display middle codependent symptoms and signs of shame, denial control, dependence (unconscious) and dysfunctional boundaries and communication. These can all lead to issues with intimacy. One study found a strong connection between narcissism and. Although the majority of Narcissists can be classified as codependents, the reverse isn't the case - codependents in their maximum aren't the narcissists. They don't display the usual characteristics of entitlement, exploitation and lack of empathy.

Dependency

Codependency is a disease of an "misplaced self." The codependent has lost their connection to their true self. Their thinking and behavior focus on a specific individual either substance, person, or. Narcissists are also afflicted by an absence of connection to their authentic personas. Because of this, they are classified as an ideal version of themselves. The lack of internal security and lack of connection to their true self makes them dependent on others to validate their existence. In turn, just like other codependents, their self image as well as their behavior are a way to maintain their stability and validate their self-worth and fragile self-image.

In a state of bliss, despite their being self-confident Narcissists seek recognition from other people and have an unstoppable desire to be recognized - in order to obtain the "narcissistic supplies." This causes them to be dependent on others' recognition since addiction is dependent in their dependence.

Shame

Shame is a part of addiction and codependency. It's a result of being raised in a dysfunctional group of family members. The self-inflated opinion of narcissists is not a good idea for self-love. Self-flattery, however, and self-conceit help to alleviate the insinuated, internalized shame which is typical of codependents.

Children develop a variety of strategies for dealing with the stress insecurity, fear, and hostility they encounter growing as children within dysfunctional family structures. Disgraceful

internalization can with no regard to the motives of the parents or there is a dearth of explicit violence. To feel secure children, they develop coping strategies which help them the necessary courage to present their best self. One strategy is to be accommodating others and seek their affection, love and acceptance. The other option is seeking fame, dominance and dominance over
others. Codependents who are stereotypical fall in the first category , and narcissists into the second. They sought out control and strength in their environments in order to have their needs met. Their search for the status of superiority, status and strength helps them stay away from feeling inadequate as well as feeling prone, dependent and powerless in any cost.

These beliefs are normal human desires, however when it comes to people who are codependents and narcissists they're compulsive , and consequently, nervous. In addition, the more one is obsessed with their ideal self, the more they are away from their true self. This can create a sense of insecurity, a false self-esteem, and feelings of shame.

Denial

Denial is a middle-level symptom of codependency. Codependents tend to be denial of their codependency, and frequently their desires and feelings. Narcissists also deny feelings, and especially those who display vulnerability. They aren't willing to admit feelings of inadequateness even to them. They shun and frequently engage in other emotions they believe are "vulnerable," which include feelings of loneliness, longing, sadness feeling powerless, guilt fear, as well as other variations. The emotion of anger can be experienced effectively. Affection, vanity, anger and contempt are all defenses against shame that are underlying.

Are you able to have a healthy relationship with an Narcissist?

My most recent dance routine with a narcissist has prompted me to conduct an audit of my relationship. In the past year, I've held myself accountable and accountable for the behavior I engage in which threaten my intellectual well-being and emotional security.

I've been guilty in the past of ignoring patterns that result in similar scenarios, where I end up involved in terrible'situation ships with men -- and the latest example is proof of this.

I now understand the pattern. In the past I've met these narcissists. But for the most part I was oblivious to their games of mind and manipulation as I was completely secluded emotionally.

When the red flags started to appear and I had an affair, but I also did not criticize them for their video games. I kept my distance and then walked out.

Boundaries are crucial in any relationship however, they're especially important with an person who is a narcissist. In any case, I continue to attract them. And in some form or manner I am able to inspire them before than I can spot what's happening.

The pathology and psychology of the narcissist isn't changed; a disgrace of guidance due to the fact that everyone deserves love and friendship and this raises the question: can you really be relationship with someone who is a Narcissist?

I'm not an expert, and I had to use my knowledge of research to determine the possibility of it. Idealism has me believing the truth that we deserve to be loved and redeemed affection because we thrive in networks and desire to be part of a community -- after all, we're here to be part of a group.

The entire literature I've read about narcissists is a blatant failure to create healthy relationships. However, as I've mentioned I'd like to believe there are some exceptions from the standard. What I've learned from my research.

The Narcissist in the relationship

Narcissists can be complex and devious people, and so having relationships with oneregardless of whether it's professional, romantic or just a casual one -- is a very loaded and confusing situation. The reason they're difficult to navigate is because sometimes, narcissists can be helpful, supportive and appear to are concerned about you, claims Wendy Behary, LCSW, author of the book Disarming The Narcissist. -- provide

It's true that they're best in their kindness and accomodation to benefit themselves, Behary says. The whole group of narcissists feeds on and fuel their egos. they make money generated by your interactions.

However, a lot of us are being in relationships that involve narcissists. it's not until you're in a deep rut and you feel you are unable to quit. While you may be able to remove yourself from an narcissist ex that is a narcissist not a simple task. The possibility of falling back is unavoidable.

"With the help of and vast, narcissists aren't equipped with the skills that make strong relationships. Particularly, empathy and regular compassion, as well as the ability to be consistent in public and compromising, kindness, reciprocity, and mutuality" Says Ramani Durvasula, Ph.D. Medical psychologist licensed by the state of California and author of I stay or should go: Surviving a courtship with a narcissist. Durvasula says. They're not "capabilities" in the sense of being however they are the reasons that narcissists are able to be in relationships. -- Supply

I had a difficult time trying to tell the story of my narcissist of the moment of my life. The lack of mutuality, empathy, the sameness, and reciprocity, left nothing to be desired. Through a series of events I outlined that I desire humans in my life to help me stay healthy and energetic.

The relationships you have with someone are investments and require mutual respect, consideration as well as information and
consideration. Narcissists' actions can reflect on the person or people they're with, but most of the time, it's not true and therefore not sustainable.

There were times when I thought that many of what he had to say to me had been fabricated and cut out of plastic jokes he's rehearsed on numerous occasions -- mostly during the love-bombing scenes.

It's true that they must feed the person or woman they are courting but only do so that will evoke adoration in order to boost their self-esteem. Performance and grandiosity suffocate all the things they say or do in the course of courting.

It's carefully crafted to the accents they put on their speech.

In the end, the actual connection to emotion and friendship with a narcissist is impossible. Yet, they're so adept at creating illusions and that's the reason they appear to be a good choice for relationships until they're not.

This means that in the end, those who are in relationships with narcissists may feel isolated, neglected and unheard and may end up appearing depressed. It's not uncommon for them to research the whole issue and feel that it's your fault for failing to keep them engaged.

They have never been in a relationship, and it hurts. I've learned this by accidentbut I do think that narcissists might be in healthy relationships?

Narcissists can certainly display Empathy?

One of the most harmful characteristics of a narcissist the total lack in empathy as well as the capacity to be genuinely concerned for other people. This is the reason why research has been conducted to investigate the possibility of triggering emotional responses from people who narcissists look at others in the event that they are taught to show empathy.

My study led me to take a look at the concept of Psychology in the present, where an investigation conducted by a focus group led to promising results in treating Narcissistic personality disorder.

Chapter 6 The Power Of Implementing Healthy Relationships

What do healthy relationships look Like?

The most significant impact in our daily lives could be how we interact with those who are closest to us. The relationships that we have with others are the foundation of our human race and form the basis of our social existence as a human being. At first, man was just like all animals, a hunter who was content to live in solitude. But, since Ancient man realized that living in a society improved the chances of survival as relationships have grown to be a large portion in our daily lives.

We have [T20] relationships because of many reasons. The purpose of relationships is to give us warmth, love, support and stability in our lives. However, not all people are able to experience these things regularly when it comes to their partners. For some, it's hard to achieve the minimum level of satisfaction. The majority of the time, this issue is caused by a lack of balance in the relationship structure they have. Childhood is an essential time that determines what the majority of our adulthood is likely to look like. Childhood psychological issues can result in severe mental issues which make it difficult for some individuals to have positive, healthy relationships.

What are healthy relationships like?

Healthy relationships are built on interdependence. This term describes the concept of two people living together, and respecting that each person is an individual deserving of all the respect that he/she deserves.

Through interdependence, two individuals with different life goals are able to meet, providing one another emotional, financial as well as social stability , while not depriving their own wellbeing, peace of mind or desires for their partner. Interdependence is the foundation of all relationships that are healthy. It is the sole guarantee that, over time, one person does not undermine the vital autonomy of another and infringe on the boundaries of their relationship.

On contrary, refers to an arrangement in which one party is dependent on the other to achieve emotional satisfaction. In many cases, the codependent party becomes dependent on the notion that the other person needs them. The "need to feel valued" could result in an unbalanced balance. Sometimes, however it is possible that the other person could be narcissistic or struggling with an alcohol or drug addiction.

Healthy relationships are essential for those who want to appreciate the everyday things in life. They offer you a solid base from which to build and push towards your goals. What are the essential features that define healthy relationships?

10 factors that contribute to an enduring relationship

Honesty and Mutual Respect

There is no way to fix an unrespectful relationship. Respect is an essential component of a good relationship. It is mandatory and required. Each of you should be able and willing to give each other full respect in all circumstances. Respect your partner's desires, fears goals, desires and personal boundaries. In the same way, it is vital that both parties are in a position to communicate what's in their minds completely. There is no way to be able to achieve 100% honesty, but the greater the level of honesty within relationships, the more likely it will last longer and provide the stability as well as security.

Genuine Affection

Every relationship that is serious must be built on the solid foundation[T21of affection, love and concern. They are the very first conditions which must be met in order for a relationship to be anyplace productive. In reality, many violent relationships begin on the same foundations , before moving out of line with the root. It can be due to various factors, however the main point is that a relationship that's which is not based on a long-lasting love will likely experience more ups than downs. Are you aware of the reason? Every relationship will be a bit sluggish at times, and each party may not be able to achieve the same level of intimacy as they did prior to. It's the only way to ensure the existence of a base love that will make sure that both parties are able to remain in touch with the real world.

Effective Communication

Communication is vital to every relationship. If a relationship fails make sure you are checking the communication. How well do you communicate in and around your relationship? Do you know how to convey the thoughts and feelings that are in your head to him? It is crucial to keep communication continuous, consistent, and clear. Effective communication can stop the development of distrust and suspicions, as well as conflicts of interest , and even a break in relationships. Even in times of conflict it is crucial to ensure that communication lines are unambiguous.

Sacrifices

The bonds of friendship can bring many benefits. Sometimes, we can gain a mentor, coach for business adviser, and confidant within one individual. But, you must be willing to give up to help their partner. A selfish partner may cause a problem for the relationship to be successful. A healthy relationship is one that has couples who are prepared to make enormous sacrifices for their partner.

Trust

A relationship that is not based on confidence is about as far away from dependence as it is possible to be. It is the most essential element for building a strong interdependent relationship. There must be no trace of distrust or bribery in a partnership that will endure for a long time. Trust lets each of the partners carry out their day-to-day routines knowing that their partner is always on their back. It also lets them be protected from suspicions and false assertions.

Sexual Compatibility

The role of sex is crucial in any relationship. It is a known reality that sex plays an important role in determining how productive the relationship will be. If a relationship is characterized by incompatibility with regards to sexual preference and desires of both partners is likely to end up in the mud. Unsatisfying one's partner could cause feelings of resentment, suspicion of each other, and emotions that can create negative emotions within the relationship.

Capability to Plan and act together

A relationship brings two distinct individuals together to work and work as a team. The performance of the relationship is dependent on their ability to be capable of working together. Do you have the ability to create plans with your teammate? Do you have the ability to transform these plans into actions with your partner? It is crucial to work in teams, as it creates bonds and a sense of unity. People who have a positive relationship can function in sync.

Engagement

To build a lasting relationship, you have to be dedicated and committed to making it successful. Good relationships require effort and honesty. Each party must be in agreement and behave as if are on the long time. Both parties must be prepared to face the challenges which are bound to pop in the future and be tolerant of the other's mistakes.

Accessibility

It is not possible to remain as people in relationships and try to have a successful relationship. It is essential to be open and available to one another, particularly when it comes to demands and conflicts. Inability to be open to your partner's needs can be a significant source of conflict and problems. Every partner should be compassionate enough to provide another an open ear whenever they require one. You should be the person they can lean on whenever they require one. By helping them out and staying open to each other can further strengthen the bond.

Realistic Expectations

Many people enter relationships with unsatisfactory expectations that are not met by their partner. I have advocated selflessness access, and dedication however, these should not be a cause of putting too much pressure on your partner, even when they seem to be to be willing. Set realistic expectations for one another and don't put your partner under excessive pressure or stress. This is almost always a disaster!

Are Your Relationships Healthy?

Of all the forms that a relationship can take, one that is plagued by toxicity and abuse is the most awful thing you can do. The most abusive relationships are those with the narcissist, as we have discussed in the book earlier as well as a codependent victim with a lost identity due to the need to meet the demands of her narcissist companion. Due to his mental state, it's easier for a narcissist play around with a codependent partner. Because of this, it is crucial for codependents to identify and stay away from harmful relationships.

Here's a list of ten characteristics that abusers of all kinds are known to carry.

Humiliation

Abusive partners love to hurt the people they share with and causing them to suffer lots of suffering. This is why they are always in the center of jokes and take the brunt of jokes. In public and in private an abusive partner might attempt to slap you to satisfy his own sense of twisted pleasure.

Power Struggles

Relationships that are abusive have many power struggles in which each person tries to gain some influence and determine the direction that the relationship will take. Even if they're only brief power struggles can be an alarming sign.

Conditional Love

Does your partner ever say things that say, "I like you but ..." to you?" Does it appear as if their love for you is contingent and determined by certain elements like appearance and intelligence in isolation? Do they make you feel as if they are an a possibility instead of a final decision? These are indications of potential misuse in the near future.

Excessive Criticism

Receiving and giving criticism is normal in a relationship with the condition that the criticism is appropriate and constructive, and it will be conveyed in a manner that will help the other grow. The way to handle criticism in a relationship that is abusive is different. It's an active type of abuse. Does your partner critique everything you perform? Does your partner make you feel like a fool by his harsh critiques of your abilities or performance? Do you receive the same level of criticism to all those in his vicinity? Or is it reserved to you only? In any event, overly negative, unsubstantiated criticism could be the catalyst for more psychological abuse.

Silence for long periods and poor communication

If your partner is in withdrawing moods over long periods of time or stops communicating periodically it is likely that you are in a relationship that is abusive. Refraining from speaking or depriving an individual of your attention is a clear sign of abuse. This is a sign that states, "I am going to act as if I do not exist in order that you might hurt me for a little."

Threats that are hidden

There's no reason the other party should be able to issue threats. If your relationship is often pushed into "threats" area chances are that you're already in a relationship that is toxic.

Blurred Boundaries

Boundaries are crucial to our well-being. They allow us to remain different and unique as individuals. They must be maintained in the event that the relationship is going to last for a long time. It is essential to respect those boundaries that are shared by all people involved. There are no limits to be crossed and each party must not lose their identity to accommodate their partner's. If you're finding it difficult to differentiate between what you desire and what your partner is looking for, you ought to rethink your relationship as it seems pretty fascinating.

Control and Dominance

Does your spouse keep track of all aspects of your daily life? Are they able to snoop on your social media accounts and accounts? Do you wish to know where you go as well as whom you talk to? Are you unreasonable in his decisions? Can you not argue an opposing opinion to the thoughts he has already in his mind? They are usually hostile and aggressive in the long term.

Cheating

If you are the victim of a cheating partner the person is making you vulnerable to some of the most severe types of abuse. Being the victim of a cheating partner is extremely disconcerting and distressing. It requires you to examine your own inner world for signs of issues that aren't there. Does your spouse have a history of being a cheater? It's a constant sign of of respect, and even violence towards you.

Try to Separate You

Some people who abuse others can be quite intelligent. Be aware that some acquaintances of yours could recognize their devious ways they might try to cut off your contact with the individuals you had the most close relationship with before you got to know them. If your partner is forcefully trying to make you feel isolated and restrict your family and friends members from your life the foundation for abuse of a larger scale could already be in place.

Chapter 7: Learn To Identify And Manage Your Triggers

Although you may not always engage in violent behavior with other people or constantly lose your temper there is a good chance that you've encountered certain circumstances and events that trigger off your narcissistic tendencies , and cause you to behave in a rude manner with other people.

In the last chapter, we spoke about watching the way you exhibit various behavior patterns that are narcissistic. In this chapter and the next step you should take that table, look it over and re-examine your triggers and look for ways to deal with them more effectively.

What situations trigger you to Be Rude?

The first step is to pay close attention to the various situations that can trigger your Narcissism. As you observe these triggers and other ones be sure to look at the root of the problem.

Are you frustrated or lose temper every time somebody says that you're incompetent? What is the reason? Do you think it's because your parents and teachers were the ones who used to label you as stupid?

Do you find yourself dismissive of others' suggestions? Do you get angry during heated debates or lose your composure when you're overwhelmed because you have a lot to manage?

Are you rude when handling the finances of others or transferring money to your father who is sick managing your business and performing a variety of tasks by yourself?

Finding the root for your triggers can be crucial for self-regulation.

Track all triggers for a particular situation and work on the following areas to better manage them:

How do you manage and control situations that trigger

Beware of situations in which you're sure that you are likely to act in a narcissistic manner. If you observe a discussion becoming a heated debate and you are unable to leave, do so prior to feeling the need to ridicule others' thoughts.

If you panic when you must deal with things due to an imminent deadline, attempt to plan your tasks prior to the deadline. Make a list of the time, date, and what to do and adhere to that plan.

Know your weaknesses Don't be embarrassed of them. If you're not great in the field of finance, it's appropriate to engage an expert in finance. If you are unable to fit certain tasks into your schedule, give the tasks to your partner. They will be grateful, both verbally and physically--for their help.

Be aware of upsetting situations that could cause narcissistic behavior. For example, if you observe someone performing a wrong act, and you have a strong desire to scream and prove that person wrong, you can distract yourself by doing something else that is more engaging.

If you begin to make these small steps and you'll soon be being more in control when you are you are in these situations.

What people trigger your Narcissistic behavior?

Beyond the specific circumstances, there could be people who trigger your self-centered behavior. For example, if you have a father who is a dictator who's orders you've always obeyed, you could show the same behaviors when you are with your spouse, coworkers or even children.

You can become quite defensive when you're around your father. Although you have to follow him, you don't have a good feeling about it and when you are around him, you're more most likely to let your anger onto your children and spouse.

Perhaps you know an acquaintance or friend who is superior to you in certain aspects. Although you don't openly acknowledge his superiority, deep in you dislike the person for it. You may subconsciously become apprehensive and aggressive around the other person and go to extreme lengths to show that you're superior.

Find out the influences that have a significant impact on your life, so that you can come up with better strategies to remain calm when they are around. Be aware of the way you react to various people, and especially people you interact with frequently.

Consider your thoughts, feelings and behave when you are with certain people. You may appear silent or rigid when you are around certain people. After having left their space, you may behave self-centered with others by venting your anger towards them.

When you have a better understanding of who is setting off your narcissism. Follow the following rules:

How do you control and manage these triggers

At first it is always recommended to stay clear of people who are causing trouble when you can. If, for instance, one of your siblings or parents is causing you to be so angry that you behave in a pompous manner in front of others, avoid interacting with them for a time. If you find a coworker who is controlling and makes you feel like a narcissist you, request your boss to assign you to a different cubicle or a team entirely.

Do not respond to messages or phone calls from those who abuse you emotionally or make fun of your appearance, and cause unhealthy NPD-related behaviors. Like we said earlier there is no naturally narcissist. It's something we are taught and our surroundings significantly impacting our behavior. If you find that certain people make you feel bad about you, stop interacting with them in any media.

Also look for the negative behaviors you want to alter within yourself. Consider how you react when you are triggered, and the reasons why you want to alter these behaviors.

Make a list of these behaviors to help you define the changes you would like to achieve. For instance, Bob, 35, was struggling with NPD. After losing a lot of his family members and realizing that he had to manage his self-centered behavior. The man realized that was in the habit of publicly devaluing those who had provoked his personality traits of narcissism. He was also known to yell at people who annoyed them and cursed them for not doing the things he wanted. In addition, he was in the habit of leaving places and restaurants when the situation didn't go according to what the way he had hoped. As with Bob in identifying the triggers you need to change is the key to becoming more emotionally at peace with yourself.

Once you've identified these behavior patterns, consider your ideal response to the scenarios you have identified What would you want to handle an event that you've previously been a victim of narcissism. In Bob's situation instead of screaming or cursing or even threatening those who provoked his anger, he would prefer to talk calmly and softly. In order to not lose his peace He also desired to speak his thoughts rationally and calmly. He was determined to not leave during an occasion, such as a celebration or dinner.

It is now time to work on delay your unwelcome behavior. This is also the case when specific events or thoughts cause you to Narcissism. The typical reaction to triggers is your present unwanted behavior, which you perform automatically. It's now embedded in your brains to become a habit. That is the reason why it's your default response. You do it while in autopilot mode.

To alter those reactive behaviors You must first be aware of the reactions. Keep track of the times and how you participate in those actions.

If you're in the presence of those who cause you to feel uncomfortable or when you encounter situations that trigger your narcissistic behavior or trigger you to feel emotions and thoughts that cause you to be narcissistic you should count up to 25 or 30 before responding.

Do five slow deep, calm, and relaxing breaths to ease your emotional impulsive behavior. Take a deep breath until you reach a number of four, and then take a deep breath, count up until four. Then breathe out and count to four . You can keep that in until you reach four. Also known as the'square (or box breathing) technique' this method helps ease the tension of an emotional storm. If you do it when you feel a strong desire to act out in a bizarre manner to an event it will help the urge to stop in a natural way.

If you're feeling more calm, think about the previous time you were in the same circumstance, where you gave in to your urges, and see what the outcome was for you. Most likely, it didn't go as planned for you and you could have ended up aggravated an already difficult situation. Consider what it would be like to give in to your desire could ruin the current situation as well.

When you talk to yourself, it's more manageable to control your impulsive responses by choosing a calm and controlled alternative.

Next step would be replacing the behavior you're trying to stop with a different approach. Following Bob's example that he was able to speak in a calm manner to people, not shouting at them. Once he was able to control the desire to yell at people, he began contemplating before speaking and speaking slowly to make some space between his thoughts and ensure that his words were not offensive. If you are a regular user of curse at someone and are determined to change this behavior, make a conscious effort to engage in this alternative way of speaking. If you'd like to replace phrases like "You are horrible," "F**"" with "I want you to realize that it is better to take this approach,"" be sure to say the phrases.

When you practice consciously the substitution responses, you gradually develop and strengthen the neuronal pathways associated with those reactions, infusing the new pathways into your brain. After several times, these routines will develop into routines that you perform in autopilot mode.

Keep a journals of your efforts to manage and control those triggers as well as reactions. Examine your behavior and performance regularly to identify your areas of focus to enhance and celebrate your accomplishments.

If you are able to stop yourself from screaming at someone, you should be happy with yourself and maybe celebrate your accomplishment by gifting yourself something nice. Rewards can help you stay on your goal, encouraging you to stick to your objectives. If you recognize yourself as acting well by tying attractive rewards to different milestones, it will make you strive to be the best you can be.

Keep in mind to be calm and gentle with yourself during this time. It took a long time to develop narcissistic behavior. Naturally, it takes time to replace the unhealthy behaviors with positive ones.

It takes between 21-90 days, but sometimes it takes longer to develop or break habits. The amount of time required depends on the nature of the habit and the extent to which it is deeply rooted.

Because manipulative behavior makes you feel strong, they provide an euphoric feeling which makes you feel happy about yourself. This is the reason why you are in a state of narcissism and have a difficult time overcoming them.

You must give yourself at least 90 days to work on these habits, and during this period you must be gentle and reassuring to yourself. There are times when you may be unable to maintain your focus in this period and you might be unable to maintain your equilibrium in certain situations. You may engage in narcissistic behaviours even though you've made a commitment to be an improved person. When this happens, stay away from being harsh with yourself.

Instead, take your time take responsibility for your mistakes, admit to the unacceptable behavior, accept responsibility for it, and then work on the principles again. Be persistent, think of your motivational reasons and envision being free from unhealthy habits. When you do this you are inspired to achieve your goals, and you will gain the determination to overcome any obstacle.

Keep in mind that narcissism can be simply a set of unwholesome behaviors and habits that you've cultivated over time. Through planning, effort and discipline it is possible to change any behavior.

While you are working on these principles, you should try to accept your feelings and be more aware of your behavior and its consequences. This will allow you to recognize your actions in a timely manner.

Let's discuss this in the next chapter:

Chapter 8: Signs That You're The Victim Of Narcissistic Abuse

Take a look at this: it's altered and distorted the entire real world. You've been brutally victimized, humiliated, and cheated or slammed, denigrated, and even screamed at to can imagine the world. The man you believed was yours was broken into millions of tiny pieces and your life was a mess together.

You've lost or diminished your self-confidence. You've been portrayed as idealized as a person, then devalued, and finally taken off the pedestal. Perhaps you've been rejected and replaced multiple times only to be kept in the dark and then dragged to a more gruelling cycle of abuse that was never there before. You might have been stalked or harassed, and threatened often to be with your abusive partner.

This was not an ordinary breakup or a relationship break-up: it was a prelude for the sly and secretive destruction of your inner mental health and confidence. But, there might not be any visible bruises to reveal the truth the only thing you'll have is fragments of broken pieces and the wounds inside from the war.

This is how narcissistic abuse appears to be.

Psychological violence of malignant narcissists can include the physical or emotional assault as well as stonewalling, poisonous manipulation, deceit, smear tactics triangulation, and different forms of intimidation and control. This can be done by someone who lacks empathy or displaying an unjust feeling of entitlement and using manipulating others to achieve their goals to the expense of other people's needs.

Due to the long-term effects of abuse, victims can be suffering from PTSD or complex PTSD symptoms, particularly if they've suffered other traumas, such as being victimized by narcissistic parents or even suffering from the known as "Narcissistic abuse syndrome" (Staggs (2016) and Stailk, 2017). The effects of narcissistic abuse could include anxiety, depression and hyper-vigilance, a numbing feeling of guilt that is toxic and psychological hallucinations that bring the victim to trauma and an overwhelming feeling of inadequacy and despair.

If we're caught trapped in an continuous cycle of abuse, it can be difficult to pinpoint exactly what is happening because the perpetrators are adept at twisting and bending reality to meet their personal needs, engaging in a ferocious love-bombing of abuse and convincing clients that they're the ones who are causing the harm.

If you are experiencing the symptoms listed below and are or were in a toxic relationship someone who is disrespectful, insinuating and shaming you, it is possible that you be the victim of an emotional predator.

1. Dissociation can be an escape mechanism.

It is possible to feel emotionally or physically isolated from the world and experience memory disruption perception, vision and self-sense. In his book"The Body Keeps the score the psychiatrist Dr. Van der Kolk (2015) states "Dissociation is the core of trauma. Experiences that are subjective get split and deformed, so that images, smells, feelings and physical sensations can take on an identity on their own. "Dissociation when confronted with terrible circumstances can result in the mind becoming numb. Because it gives you an escape from your current realities, mind-numbing routines like addictions, obsessions and even deprivation could be a habit of your life. The subconscious finds ways to mentally block out the impact of pain so that you don't have to face the phobias that plague you.

It is also possible to create internal "parts" that are traumatized which are separated from your perpetrator or family members' identities (Johnston 2017, 2017). These internal parts could include those parts of an child that have not been nurtured, the true frustration and disdain you feel towards your adversaries, or parts of yourself that you aren't able to express.

Based on the work of therapist Rev. Sheri Heller (2015), "Integrating and recovering dissociated and unowned personality traits is dependent on creating a coherent narrative that permits the integration of cognitive, emotional, and physiological reality." This internal integration can be most effective with the assistance of an experienced therapist who is trauma-informed.

2. The eggshells are your walking shoes.

One of the most common signs of trauma is the inability to tolerate any activity that brings back memories of the past trauma, whether it's risk, a location or conduct. It doesn't matter if it's your friend or your girlfriend, a your family member, coworker or your employer, you're always looking at what you're doing and engaging in with that person to ensure that you don't attract the ire of their enemies, or retaliation or fall victim to their jealousy.

But you discover that this doesn't work but you remain the victim of abusers who feels right to make use of you as a punching bag for emotional reasons. You are always anxious to provoke your abuser in any waypossible, in turn, you are able to avoid confrontation or establish limits.

Outside of the abusive relationship you could also increase your behavior to please others, and get rid of the desire to be informal or assertive when you are exploring the world outside, particularly with the same people as the person who harasses you and your abuser.

3. You must put aside your essential necessities, while sacrificing your mental and physical security to satisfy the abuser.

At one point, you were filled with life, driven by purpose and dream-driven, however, today you're living to meet the needs of another and goals. The entire existence of the narcissist seemed revolve around you. Now everything revolves around you.

You might have put your dreams or interests, relationships and safety for yourself off to ensure your abuser's marriage remains' satisfied.' It is likely that you will discover, naturally that your abuser will never be completely satisfied with what you do or do not do.

4. You are struggling with health issues that are causing your mental anxiety.

It is possible that you have gained or lost substantial quantity of pounds, experienced grave health issues that were not present prior to, and have experienced the onset of physical signs of aging. The strain of continuous use has increased the cortisol levels in your body as well as your immunity system was severely impacted which makes you more vulnerable to illness and illness (Bergland 2013, 2013).

If you do, you'll have trouble sleeping or suffer from nightmares that are terrifying and reliving the experience through mental or physical flashbacks that bring you back to the initial area of wound (Walker 2013).

5. There is a general feeling of distrust.

Every person is now the threat of another and you're becoming worried about the intentions of other people in particular after witnessing the person you used to trust in the unsavory actions. Be vigilant and alert. Because the manipulative culprit has put in a lot of effort to make you believe your perceptions are not true, it is difficult to be able to trust anyone else or even you.

6. Suicidal thoughts are a common occurrence. self-harming tendency.

There is a feeling of despair, with anxiety and depression. The conditions were too difficult and even if you tried to, you were unable to run. There is a feeling of insufferable helplessness, which can make you feel like you'd rather not have another chance to live. In order to deal with this with the stress, you might even indulge in self-harm.

The SAMHSA's suicide prevention division head Dr. McKeon (2014) states that victims of violence from their intimate partners are twice as likely to commit suicide several times. This is how criminals commit murder with no trace of the law of nature.

7. Self-isolation is a process that you self-isolate.

A majority of abusers exclude their victims, however those who suffer are also isolated because they are ashamed of their own abuse. With the stigma of victim-blaming and the misperceptions about psychological and emotional violence in the society, survivors could be subject to retrauma by police, acquaintances, family members, and even the narcissist's harems that could invalidate their memories of abuse.

We worry that nobody will be able to comprehend or accept them, therefore we try to avoid other people in order to staying out of the judgment of their abusers and anger, instead of asking for assistance.

8. You begin to compare yourself to other people, usually to the point of blame yourself for the mistreatment.

Narcissistic abusers are highly skilled at creating triangles of love , or in placing another person in the relationships to make it harder for the victim even more. This is why those who suffer from narcissistic abuse experience the fear of not being satisfied , and they may try to compete to get the attention and love of the perpetrator.

The victims of good, stable marriages may be prone to comparing themselves to other people or be concerned if their spouse appears to treat other people with respect. They may be tempted to go through the trapdoors, "Why me? "And stuck within the pit of self blame. It is true that the person who did the wrong is the person to blame-you do not have any responsibility to be victimized in any way.

9. Self-sabotage is self-destructing and self-sabotage.

Victims often think about the incident and can hear voices of their perpetrator inside their minds which can amplify their self-defeating and negative self-talk tendencies. Malignant narcissists ' code' to making their victims self-destructive-sometimes to the extent of pushing them to suicide.

Victims tend to blame themselves for their own actions because they feel such guilt as a result of the blatant and covert slurs of the narcissist and the verbal violence and hypercriticism. They are deprived of their dreams and ambitions as well as their academic goals. The abuser has created an attitude of inadequacy them , and they start to believe that all good things aren't worth their weight in gold.

10. It is difficult to do the things you love, and not achieving success.

Because some predators are obsessive and envious of the prey they hunt, they get paid for their accomplishments. They cause their victims to mix with cruel and savage behavior their happiness as well as their desires, skills and the fields of success. The manipulation of their victims causes them to be averse to success so long as they're not punished with shame and punishment.

The result is that victims feel depressed, unsecure or lacking confidence. As a result, they might flee the spotlight, allowing their criminals to "steal" the show repeatedly and over. Be aware that the person who is abusing you doesn't undermine your talents since they truly believe they are superior to you It is because they're trying to take away their power over you.

11. You can protect yourself from abusers and you can even gaslight yourself.

Rationalization or minimization and the denial of abuse are typically victim's survival mechanisms in a relationship that is abusive. To minimize the dissonance in your brain that occurs when you're abused by someone who says they love you, those who suffer abuse are convinced that the perpetrator isn't really "all awful" and that the abuser have committed an act to "provoke" the violence.

It is crucial to minimize the cognitive dissonance that occurs in the opposite direction by studying the personality of a narcissist and the ways to abuse them; that means you can distinguish the present reality with the false self-image of the narcissist by understanding that the manipulative personality is the real person not their friendly façade.

Remember that there is usually an intense distress relationship between the perpetrator and victim since the victim is educated' to depend on the perpetrator to live (Carnes Carnes, 2015). Victims can defend their abusers against legal consequences, display an optimistic image of the relationship on social media or compensate for abuse by'sharing the responsibility.'

I've been victimized by narcissism. What now?

If you're in a troubled relationship you should know that you think you're all on your own. All over the world millions of people have been through what you're experiencing. There isn't a race, gender, language, religious or social class specific to this kind that is psychological torture. First step becoming aware and believe in the reality of your situation-even in the event that the perpetrator is trying to convince you otherwise.

If you can, look into your experiences in order to understand the causes that led to the brutality. Talk about the situation with a trusted expert on psychological health. They can also be advocates for domestic violence and relatives, friends or victims. Continue to heal your body through methods like yoga that is focused on trauma as well as meditation on the mind, both practices which target the same areas in the brain frequently infected from stress (van der Kolk 2015.).

Seek help if you experience some of these signs, including suicidal thoughts. Seek out a trauma-informed psychotherapist who understands the symptoms of trauma and can to guide you. Make a security plan if your adversary is violent.

Due to the strong trauma bonds that may form and the effects of trauma and the overwhelming feeling of despair and helplessness which can arise from abuse, it's difficult to get out of the abusive relationships. In the event of co-parenting you need be aware that it is possible to get out and begin your journey towards No Contact or Low Contact. It can be difficult to recover from this type of abuse, however it's worthwhile to get back to freedom and putting all the pieces back together.

Chapter 9: Attitudes And Behaviors

Let's look at the indicators to tell if someone is the signs of a Narcissist.

What are the signs to tell if a person is a narciss The signs that should not be missed

Here are some tips to spot narcissists in just one glance. Now let's discuss the typical behavior that make them distinct.

He is eager to be loved by everyone and loves being the spotlight.

There is no way to be everything to everyone It's just a fact however, narcissists aren't happy about it. They'll certainly have a long time talking about themselves and trying to impress the people present with their tales and their amazing talents. They are often apathetic and in a setting that is crowded, they'll find it easier to hide their heads down when they feel isolated and will try to find ways to be noticed. What a shame not to listen their opinions and let them feel a little pampered!

He only talks about himself and doesn't listen to other people.

Conversation with a narcissist can be something that is almost impossible to do as he will only talk about his own life and experiences. If you attempt to talk with him, he'll pretend to show an interest however only for a few minutes and will never appear genuine. After a few minutes, he will quickly be ready to interrupt you and give his opinion or talk about something similar to something that occurred to him that was resolved in a remarkable method. The narcissist will not accept that attention isn't on him, and will always shift the focus to himself and speak about his achievements.

He is always willing to critique

Even when there isn't a need, the narcissist is a critic, usually exaggerated and out of line and ready to be used by other people to hear. In everything he does , he thinks he is the best and thinks he is more intelligent than everyone else. To his belief in superiority, he also has the lack of empathy and habit of stomping on others without respect. He is so certain of himself that people who are not like him are always mistaken. When someone is too confident and confident, they end with a negative view of other people. Beware, the narcissist is likely to do it in all circumstance.

He would like to always be satisfied

If the narcissist is doing an act of greatness, the reason is for the sake of impressing others, to be appreciated and praised for his exemplary traits: in short the narcissist uses others for satisfaction. The narcissist wants others to always be thankful to him and is expecting only the best treatment from everyone. Everyone should always be able to fulfill his desires and not have to do anything for them. He is the center of the universe and makes use of people so when they're willing to please him. Otherwise, he could go without them in a flash of an eye.

He is charismatic and charming (but only for a short time)

Although narcissists are often irritating, they're also brimming with a captivating appeal. They are able create a woman feel loved and are always able to win their admirers. But, they're attracted to people to satisfy their own desires and their desire is not always true. It is a fleeting feeling that will fade once they no longer get the kind of attention he would like and helps increase confidence in himself. Additionally, after a few minutes after he realizes that there is another on hand, he'll get bored and look for more victories in order to get new proofs.

He is an expert manipulator

If you meet someone who is a narcissist, you'll be drawn to his self-professed ego and irresistible personality and that's the reason you'll be tempted to follow his desires. Through his method of conduct, the things he does, he can manipulate others and so they do whatever he wishes. In addition, many narcissists delight in creating negative emotions like guilt or sadness to others, as a means to attract attention to themselves. They are also able to play up their emotions when they are subjected to criticism. They will cause us to feel guilty for having they made them feel guilty They can respond with aggression or even lock themselves completely silent. This is a method of reactivity which is often damaging in the long run.

Feels unique

As per one of the narcissists every person he meets would be in danger without his help. He's so happy that he believes that he is unrivaled. He is a person with no rival and believes that those who surround him cannot exist without him and his help. An example of this is: "if it were not me, no one would be able to accomplish anything".

He is envious and loves creating jealousy

The biggest problem with people who believe too much in their own self-worth? They love provoking the admiration of others. in their perception, it's proof that they live a flawless life. They are also jealous of the achievements of others. I believe that I am deserving one and that I are the only one who get to enjoy certain advantages. Talk with a narcissist over one of your goals, the narcissist will minimize it in a matter of seconds to talk about his feat , and then to prove that he is astonished by his excellence.

He is not mature and doesn't admit to his mistakes.

Although he will try to prove his strength and perfection the narcissist has many flaws. He is extremely childish emotionally in the sense that the narcissist could take any action to prove his superiority. They are also not willing to admit that they're wrong according to their own opinion, everything they do is flawless.

Consider the companion as an accessory that makes him a victim and unsecure

The narcissist can be uncaring in relationships with others and is not a great friend to their partner, considering them to be a minor part of their lives. He will always find an opportunity to smear the other person, making him feel insecure, to the point that he's incapable of doing anything without his own opinion. He's also the master of blame. He constantly finds a way to blame his partner , while the benefits of the situation, when they are good will always be his.

10 subtypes and types of Narcissism

Does narcissism actually constitute an all-encompassing disorder? Absolutely yes.

The most reliable estimation was made in 2010 when an investigation was conducted and it was revealed that narcissistic disorders can cause a 6% or more in the general population. Furthermore, the study suggests a higher rate of incidence in the male population. Although this percentage is acknowledged as such, is actually under-estimated.

According to an Meta study conducted at the end of 2015 found that narcissism is seen as growing more prevalent, particularly among the younger generations. It's evident it is a very real and clearly a current issue.

While it is true that narcissism can be an extremely widespread disorder however, it's equally real that there are numerous kinds of narcissism that are classified by different writers based on various guidelines. In the most popular definitions, the narcissist is an untrustworthy person as well as chameleonic and Machiavellian. However, we'll see that this isn't always the case.

Different subtypes of Narcissism:

"To create a bundle from every grass"

Making a bundle from the whole weed This cliche can be a little symbol of what's happening with Narcissism.

It is a sign of the attitude of those who, when faced with a particular subject tend to overgeneralize, and don't consider (voluntarily or unintentionally) the distinctions and differences between different kinds of "grass" they claim to put together into one "bundle". Narcissism is one of them but that's how the Diagnostic and Statistical Manual of Mental Disorders does too, and it's a pattern that's partially to blame.

Narcissistic personality disorders are extremely complex and includes a variety of different aspects. In fact, it could be stated that there are several subtypes of pathological Narcissism.

While the subtypes aren't listed on the Diagnostic Manual (DSM V) I have listed below the five subtypes of pathological narcissism identified in the work of Theodore Million, an American psychologist renowned for his work on personality disorders.

1. Unscrupulous Narcissist

Displays characteristics of an Antisocial Personality Disorder.

It's sort of the equivalent of our perverse Narcissist. It's got outstanding characteristics of an antisocial personality which be in conflict with his personality disorder. He is not remorseful and is arrogant, naive as well as manipulative and vindictive and does not possess morals or the least respect for other people. His character is similar to that of a psychopath and, in a small way, the sociopath's.

2. Compensation Narcissist

Presents avoidant personality disorder traits.

It's probably the most susceptible subtype. The person who suffers from it compensates for low self-esteem issues with an assumption that he is better than other people. He believes that he is special and exceptional and may also possess traits of personality that are shared with avoidant personality disorders.

3. Seductive Narcissist

Shows signs of the the disorder known as histrionic personality.

To the personality disorder that is his primary Are there additional personality traits that are characterized by histrionics? This is one who is a narcissist, who wants to be the center of attention and will go to all measures to be at the center of focus. He's an insidious liar, flatterer , and engages in sexually sexually sexy, flirtatious behavior.

4. Elite narcissist

It's a variant that is a variation of "pure model" however there is a distinct tendency to social climb. He believes he is entitled, however his façade has nothing to relate to reality. He is looking for a comfortable and facilitated life and has a worry of becoming "normal".

5. Pure narcissist

It meets the diagnostic criteria of DSM V and lacks histrionic or antisocial personality characteristics. He is not compassionate or empathy. The relationships that he is able to create lack reciprocity. and he has high standards and feels unique, and is hoping to be acknowledged by other people. He is an "natural predisposition" to the leadership position, is highly competitive, and as with any type of narcissists, has a tendency to manipulate.

Short classification

There are many authors who have devoted themselves to the study of different types of Narcissism. For instance, we have:

1. Paranoid Narcissist

Displays characteristics of paranoid personality disorder.

As with all kinds of narcissists person is also apathetic is arrogant and contemptuous towards other people and worries that, due to jealousy or other motives other people might criticize him or cause harm to him in different ways.

2. Narcissist hedonist

It's a blend of the four primary subtypes of narcissistic Millon. It's possible to alternate between stages and fluctuate, meaning it is in one sense prone to rejection, and vulnerable as those who are compensatory, yet lavish as the elitist type. If he adopts a self-defying manner, or he may decide to be isolated from the world or, in the opposite, require to be the histrionic or seductive kind of.

3. Malignant narcissist

It's very similar to Millon's original subtype of narcissists, which means that even in this case there are distinct antisocial traits in the personality, however additionally, there might be personality traits that are paranoid and an inclination to be sadistic.

The most well-known classification is: covert and overt

His theory by Wink (1991) is certainly the most popular, therefore I put it aside for the my final post. The author proposed the existence of two distinct kinds of narcissism: the both covert and overt. The narcissist who is overt thinks of being superior in self-esteem, self-reliance in control and control over other people while the covert narcissist exhibits emotions like anger and shame, and is haunted by the fear of being in constant disarray which can lead to the anxiety of being rejected by others. Let's take a look at all the details.

Narcissism that is overt

The narcissist who is overtly observant has an impressive self-esteem as well as a poor tolerance to criticism. Are able to maintain a safe or devaluing attitude and less anxiety when it comes to social interactions. Also, he displays an obvious emotional distancing and criticizes emotional bonds in a way that he avoids them due to the possibility of compromising the self-worth of his character. The most prominent characteristics of open Narcissism are the same ones that in the other categories embodied the PURE subtype. They include the superiority and contempt obsessed with success, the need to control or rule and absence of empathy superficial and ineffective social connections.

Covert narcissism

The narcissist who is hidden, in contrast is sensitive to criticism, constantly thinks about and has low self-esteem. The attachment style is afrightening and is characterized by constant anxiety that is followed by the avoidance of relationships.

The person who is narcissist in covert mode has an unending fear of rejection or abandonment when it comes to relationships. The person who is portrayed as covert can be described as a vulnerable, introverted person and extremely sensitive. The sensitivity of this person is mostly related to judgement and is often criticized by those around him; he is afraid of self-doubt and will defend himself in any subject that could challenge his decisions. He has a tendency to idolize other people.

However, even in the form of covert narcissism there's no deficiency of grandiose feelings that are more difficult to recognize since they're disguised under shyness, introversion , and depressive symptoms. The person who is a covert narcissist may have difficulty maintaining a relationship over a long period of time and may also have characteristics that are similar to Borderline personality disorders (precisely because of the pronounced fear of being abandoned) and an overly critical attitude to others as well as himself.

Similarities between covert and open Narcissism

In both their overt and the covert form, narcissists crave for admiration and constant adoration as well as fantasies of grandeur the feeling that all of their success is due to them ... Narcissists of both types increase self-esteem by admiring others, and are inclined to manipulate and arrogance. Both types are arrogant but the assumption of concealment is greater and they are more critical (the covert can be a problem for itself) and they ignore the needs of other people because they are unable to recognize their needs and might have difficulties in controlling their urges (especially when their profiles contain traits of borderline personalityand are marked by a high degree of behavioral and emotional unstable).

Both kinds of narcissists display an impressive appearance, however the ways they express themselves vary. The open-faced are grandiose and arrogant in order to disguise depression and insecurity. Contrarily, the coverts are shy and insecure to conceal the grandiose inner.

Correlation between Narcissism and the other disorders

Yet, according to research that show narcissistic personality disorders have the highest rate of co-morbidity with other mood or behavior disorders, including dissociative, depressive eating disorders bipolar disorder, and most importantly, the use of drugs.

Chapter 10: Narcissist's Object

Narcissists, as with all abusers, have a favorite "victim" who they pursue. The victims tend to be the most likely to meld into the narcissist's story which allows them to make up their own reality. If you're engaged to someone who is a narcissist, you might be wondering what led you to this situation.

"Why do I feel this way?" is a massive question that people who have been hurt will have to. Perhaps you are feeling as if the narcissist picked you due to something fundamentally wrong about you. You could also feel like there's something wrong with your character because you weren't able to anticipate the abuse, and you begin to feel embarrassed in your self. Believe that the fact that you are a victim isn't your fault. It's not because you have something wrong with you in any way. The narcissist might have realized that you're extremely compassionate compassion, loving, and caring and tried to manipulate you into becoming an untrue reality.

However, there are some qualities and characteristics that all victims share at least to a certain extent. These are the most commonly-used characteristics that are found on resumes of victim of narcissism.

Conscientiousness

One of the most under-appreciated traits that a narcissist can display is their conscientiousness. Narcissists are aware that if someone is a conscientious person, they are more likely to keep their word in their promises and usually assume that the narcissist is likely to be the same. In turn, they can take advantage of this characteristic to make the victim be served directly by them.

Someone who is mindful tends to give others the benefit of doubt. They tend to give second chances, and eventually become a part of the actions of the narcissist. Because they are willing to accept second chances and recognize the good in the narcissist. The person who is a narcissist understands that they could take advantage of this and turn someone who is conscientious into a victim of an unending desire to satisfy. If you're exceptionally likable and conscientious, you possess the ideal traits for an narcissist to mold you to meet their requirements. They will profit from you, repeatedly robbing your character and ruining your life as you continue to that you see the best in them. In the pursuit of to see the positive in other people, you're less likely to recognize the person you perceive to be a narcissist really are. They thrive in this kind of environment because it implies that you are not only not seeing them as they really are, you're not even looking for it. You'd rather find the positive in these people and grant them the benefit doubt, rather than acknowledge to anyone else or yourself that they're acting for no other motive other than love or misguided efforts to show love.

Empathy

Being able to empathize is an essential requirement if you're going to be a target for the narcissist. They are attracted to the empathy of their victims, and it means you're likely to be incredibly easy to manipulate. For them, this is your biggest weakness and it could become the most powerful tool against you. Since a narcissist is a person who craves and seeks attention as well as praise and encouragement from others, they rely on people with an incredibly high level of empathy. They are much more likely to give the attention they require in order to feel comfortable.

If you are a person who is empathetic is more likely to understand what you feel and, as a consequence you will act in accordance with the emotions you feel rather than what you're viewing. If you're a narcissist, this is the perfect situation. Since they're feeling an immense amount of hurt and suffering deep within They know that you are able to sense it and they will pleasure in their suffering. And then, they play with that pity to extract what they want from you. They also make use of your empathy aspect to diminish you because they know that you are guided by your emotions. The ones who are guided by their emotions are more prone to manipulation since all the narcissists have to play is with your emotions and create an atmosphere of guilt, shame, and discontent inside you. Once they've accomplished that, they are able to decide when you feel happy and when you do not.

Another benefit of being compassionate is that you'll listen to their stories of pain and feel their pain. They'll try to trick you into believing they are victims but you must verify their motives and be sure that you be in their shoes and that you'll wish to keep them from becoming the victim. They are aware that you are inclined to accept forgiveness as you seek to see the positive in people. This is only a further confirmation of their belief that you're incapable of "think" about yourself and allows the narcissists to control you by manipulating your feelings and then force your thoughts to conform to their desires.

If you're a sensitive and empathetic individual, commonly known as an Empath it means you are motivated through your feelings more strongly than an typical person. Not only are you able to connect to how the other is experiencing however, you are able to feel it too. This means you're much more likely to accept what they say and provide them with the things they want because you desire to make them feel better. However, they will never be because they really cannot. If you're an Empath one could be more vulnerable to physical abuse due to your nature. You are blessed with the one thing that a Narcissist is lacking the most empathy. They attract you like moths flock to the flame.

If you think you're an Empath and you want to know more about what it means and how to defend yourself, look up the book I wrote: "Highly Sensitive Empaths: The Complete Guide to Self-discovery, protection against Narcissists as well as Energy Vampires, and Developing the Empath Gift."

Integrity

Narcissists who are morally poor are very attracted by one who is dependable with their words. If you're honest and integrity, you possess a wealth of attributes that a narcissist could use for profit. A lot of people with integrity are not willing to violate their moral code, or even give up on the relationship. It is much easier for a narcissist to keep their partner in the relationship until they are not capable of leaving due to the psychological harm that they have caused.

Narcissists do not feel any remorse for the harm they cause to their victims. But, their victims typically be reluctant to risk morally responding in any way. A victim with high convictions, is not willing to break up the relationship or abandon the obligations they believe they owe to the person who is a narcissist. Integrity can be beneficial to those who are involved in a relationship with similar-minded people, but for those who are engaged with a narcissist may keep them in the relationship for many years.

Resilience

Resilient individuals is able to endure difficult situations. The narcissist plays on the strength of the victim to increase the bonds that exists between the person who is the victim as well as the perpetrator. It might seem counterintuitive however, it serves the narcissist in an enormous way. People who are not capable of dealing with the abuse tend to quit their relationship soon. People who are able to "toughen to" the abuse tend to stay in the relationship since they heal between episodes and, as they believe, deal with the incidents as they occur. If a victim decides to leave the relationship, after having realized the extent of how toxic or abusive the relationship is, a person who has a high level of resiliency will rebound after their period of separation.Most victims come back hoping that things will get better. If they aren't The victim will know the core of their being that they are strong enough to stand up against the violence.

Resilience is a vital quality to possess that will help you overcome adversity and reaching your goals in your life. However, when it's been twisted to suit the needs of the narcissist, it could turn into a weapon of pain which strengthens the bonds you have with the person who is abusive and can make you more reluctant to end the relationship. Someone who is resilient is more likely to disregard their urge to leave, preferring to fight to the death. They could take on one or the other of these mindsets one of an aggressor, or of an saver. Whatever the mentality that the victim chooses to adopt and why, it's often employed to try to sustain the insanity-filled relationship.

Due to the trauma connection which the victim has in the relationship with the toxic person the victim could end up measuring their love based on the level of cruelty they will endure. The phrases "you always lies to me and yet you're still here, do you measure that as a sign in love?" may cross your thoughts or even your lips during discussions if you're an individual who is resilient and are caught up in the terrifying relationship between the abuser and the narcissist victim.

Weak Boundaries

People with weak boundaries are admired by the narcissist as it implies that they are less likely to exploit and remain within their circle. Individuals who are strong in their boundaries can sway the narcissist, preventing them from being able to abuse them, and then leaving after they realize that the relationship is unhealthy. But, those with weak boundaries struggle to keep people from mistreating them. That means they have a tolerance to abuse, which makes it easier for the narcissists to drag them into the vicious cycle and keep them in the cycle.

If you're someone who has difficulty enforcing boundaries or doesn't know the signs of healthy boundaries it can make you a desirable potential target for the Narcissist. This is made even more apparent when your weak boundaries are directly related to the way you allow others to speak to you and how they treat you. If you let others betray you, make a profit of you, or make you feel unwelcome because you're not sure about what to do or are already feeling weak in their presence it means that you're already a prime target for abuse. A lack of boundaries could connect to the next thing we will discuss, co-dependency.

Co-Dependent

A lot of people don't realize that they're already codependent. If you're already dependent an narcissist can detect this and immediately use to gain advantage. The main goal of a narcissist's is creating a person who is completely dependent upon them for almost everything. If you're already taught to be dependent, this implies that they don't need to force you into a relationship and is easy for them to do their job. Instead, they need to get you to commit you in their web (or the web they have created). The most difficult portion of their work is over, which makes it simpler for them to engage you.

The most common signs for codependency that psychopaths be looking for in potential victims are the victim first messaging them most of the time and asking them to hang out often and being compelled to be more open than is normal for the beginning of relationships, and looking for approval and validation from the Narcissist. The needy, overly-invested behavior indicates that you are likely to be codependent, making you a prime victim. The narcissist doesn't have to work hard to get you more involved in the relationship. This makes it much easier for the person who is narcissistic to keep you within their circle and continue engaging you as a narcissistic source.

Affectionate or sensitive Romantic

Individuals who are viewed as being sensitive or passionate romantics are favored by the self-centered narcissist. They are easily attracted by the love-bombing stage, which aids the narcissist in hooking them and keep them committed to the relationship. Because many people do not feel as romantic as the romantic is and even fewer are curated to the person in question, they become easy to be targets. Narcissists can explore what makes you feel love and what they can do to charm you and what it would be like to get you off your feet. They then tailor the love-bombing stage to your needs. By utilizing this skill to create the ideal love-filled scene that you want, the sexual narcissist becomes adept at luring you into.

Since you're sensitive This also means that you feel pain and heartbreak more than the average person. The narcissist knows this and is aware that it is difficult for you to let them go compared to the average person. So long as they create the burden of leaving harder than you are able to endure, they'll be certain that you won't ever be leaving anytime in the near future. In the process they increase their control over you and continue to use you as a narcissistic source.

Sentimentality

Another characteristic that narcissists seek to see in people is the high level of emotional attachment. People who tend to cherish their relationships are more likely to be able to bond quickly and deep with the narcissist which makes their abuser-victim relationship stronger. Narcissists are generally known to beg their victims to love them by appealing to their desire to establish a the most intimate and enduring relationship with their loved one. This is the method they use to lure their victims into the beginning phases of their relationship. This helps the narcissist gain the trust, love and loyalty of the other person early in the relationship.

The narcissist can exploit the person's emotions to make pleasant memories that the victim will love and keep for the duration of the time when abuse is taking place. This helps them look for the positive in the narcissist. This results in them being more likely to accept their abuser and see it as an unfortunate day or an error.

When a person is convicted and is obsessed with their narcissist the narcissist begins to hide emotions and withdraw in order to cause feelings of sadness and depletion within the victim. The victim then begins to panic to try to hold on and try to make things "better." The narcissist tend to rationalize and justify their behaviour, and avoid punishment, and defend the perpetrator if the victim's first reaction is full of happiness with positive feelings to keep.

The recipe of the Perfect Target

A person who has all or a majority of the traits mentioned above is an ideal candidate for a narcissist be able to exploit and take advantage of for their own games. All of these traits work to create an individual that is more prone to abuse and remains within the cycle. These individuals are much more likely accept and overcome the violence, they are less likely to develop deep relationships with, and can continue to be a lover of the narcissist, and satisfy their desire for attention, love to be loved, admired, and praised.

If you have these characteristics you have a high chance they were used to harm you. Unfortunately, the majority of these are good qualities that any person can have. When used in a healthy environment they aid your pursuit of a connected, prosperous, and thriving life that could have positive results. If misused by an abuser they could quickly turn into instruments that are employed against you.

As opposed to creating an positive bond, they serve to create an unnatural relationship with the person who is a narcissist. Instead of encouraging success, they serve to make you feel less valuable and hinder you from reaching any level of success within your own life. Instead of giving you the potential to succeed they serve to drain the life of you. Narcissists are extremely adept in utilizing your most desirable traits and traits to transform them into the worst nightmares you've ever had. This is the reason they are extremely powerful. They're sly about it, and they'll take advantage of you in all the appropriate methods to keep you entertained and returning for more.

Do not allow this to discourage anyone in any manner. Be aware of it, as the first step towards ending the narcissist's influence and beginning your path towards recovery.

Chapter 11: Contacting A Narcissist In A Relationship

Before you begin discussing the subject, it is important to be aware that many people exhibit Narcissistic tendencies. If you can identify the true narcissist in a person, you can stay clear of these individuals and handle people you already know efficiently. Consider if the person:

He is a bit over-confident of his importance.

You are expecting appreciation and attention from others.

Does not seem to care about the needs or opinions of other people;

is arrogant or superior to other people.

Believes that he is special in some way , and only extraordinary people be able to comprehend him;

He believes that others are jealous of him.

He swindles others to obtain what he wants;

is obsessed with achieving an extraordinary amount of power, fame, or the perfect love.

Find out what your needs are

If you require someone to provide an understanding and mutual support It is best to cut down on the amount of time spent with the person who is narcissist, and concentrate on other people who will provide more than you want. However when the narcissist seems to be an active and exciting person in many ways and you don't require any additional help, support, or friendship, this type of relationship could work the moment. It is important to ensure that you're not putting yourself in danger by staying in contact with the person who is a narcissist. This is particularly true when you have a strong relationship with them (such as parents or spouses) because it can consume the majority of your time and cause mental instability.

If you're tired of satisfying their needs (constant praise, validation or attention and never-ending patience) Then you have reconsider your relationship with them.

If he is abusive to your (he manipulates you speaks to you with a sense of superiority, and acts as if you're not worth anything) You must quit immediately, as it can be dangerous to your mental and emotional well-being.

Accept their limitations

If the person you are talking to is important to you, you must to admit the narcissism of this person. Do not ask the person who is narcissistic for attention or support that he's not able to provide. It will result in nothing more than irritating and dissatisfying you, something that can only harm the relationship.

For instance, if you suspect you know that Robert is narcissistic, you should not try to keep telling him how you feel, as the person who is narcissistic will not empathize and will rapidly change the direction of the conversation to him.

Other methods can be used to define your self-esteem

At the very least, self-esteem is developed from within rather than depending on external help. However, for many, it's boosted when people affirm their worth by affirming their worth as individuals. But, don't seek out a narcissist if you seek this kind of help since it will not be offered.

Remember that, even if trusting this person, they are unable to evaluate the seriousness of your issues. They may use this knowledge to manipulate your feelings, therefore be cautious about what you say to a narcissist.

Remember that the mantra of a narcissist will be "Me first." If you have to deal with this person, you'll have to act according to this principle.

Try to be compassionate.

It's easier to say it than actually doing it, however, keep in mind that, despite the supposed confidence that the narcissist displays however, he is a complete lack of trust and demands the constant approval of other people. In addition, the narcissist will not have a complete life as he is incapable of expressing the many emotions.

It doesn't mean that you should allow him to be what he wishes with you. This means that you should keep in mind that the narcissist an individual who is unable to connect to other people. It is often due to having parents who are narcissistic or prolonged experience of trauma in childhood (ie. physical, emotional or sexual assault over a prolonged period of time from one parent or both parents, or an individual).

Be aware that narcissists are unable to comprehend unconditional love. Every action they take is designed to achieve what is best for them, which can be an insular way of life. It's possible to feel empathy when you realize that their negative behaviors are manifestations of self-deprecation as well as feelings of inferiority.

Beware of mind games.

A lot of narcissists engage in mind games that require you to remain defensive constantly and increases their confidence. The best method to handle these kinds of mind games is to identify these games and cease playing. To combat an egotist, it is important to let go of your self-esteem.

Get out of the "blame game"

". Narcissists cannot commit any wrongdoing in his own mind and therefore, he requires an individual to be blamed for all of his mistakes. Someday this person is likely to be you. If you don't want to talk about or justify why it's not your fault or alter your mood and feelings, you should set boundaries. Keep an eye on what he's done in order to be able to say (in an unassuming voice), "Last Tuesday you have done xxxxxx." But, even when confronted with this fact, the narcissist will not be honest and admit they were wrong. They might say that they're a failure or aren't doing anything right however, that's an excuse to you to convince them that they're always right. They can't help it, and cannot see it.

Narcissists can be great fools. If you can recall something different from the person who is narcissistic (especially in the event that you put him in the wrong place) Don't begin to doubt your beliefs. But, don't try to argue until you've got the complete empirical evidence that shows you're correct. Even in this case, a narcissist might attempt to turn the situation in his favor.

One of the most crucial things to keep in mind is to develop an attitude of not responding to the person. If you are a victim of someone who is narcissistic, keep your eyes on the fact that they may be insults, humiliation, and deceit. Don't answer. It's like playing catch but you don't have to catch the ball to throw it over again. Don't let the game (insults or mind games etc.) be a part of the past.

Since the NARCISSIST HAS A LARGE EGO and an extremely distorted perception of HIMSELF and others, you will likely see yourself as someone who is, in a way, inferior. You might be able to win the NARCISSIST'S favor in the short term, but DO NOT EVER GUARANTEE TO SUCCESS OR impress him in the long ROUND.

Don't consider their criticism to be serious, making yourself aware that they are the result of an unbalanced viewpoint. Don't even attempt to discuss your strengths with the person you are arguing with because he won't be able listen to you.

If the narcissist is constantly vilifying you (whether it's your spouse, father, or even your boss) Find someone you trust to tell them the things he's told you (a trusted counsellor, friend or a psychologist, etc.). If you're able to, move away from him a bit so you can get back from his critiques.

Listen a lot.

If you must relate to a narcissist, the most effective way to handle it is simply to pay attention carefully. The narcissist is likely to ask for to hear and pay attention and will likely be rude or disengage if you do not want to give them. Naturally, everything has limits. If the narcissist is demanding your attention at a moment which you're not able to offer it, you should not yield. If you are planning to keep a friendship or any other connection with a narcissist must prepare yourself to hear the narcissist.

If you find yourself losing your focus Ask him to explain the last detail you've remembered to allow you to resume the the conversation. For instance, you could write "I am thinking of the things you've said about X but I couldn't understand what you had stated. Can you tell me what you said?

As honest as you can and be kind to your colleagues

The narcissist will likely have a quality you admire.make sure to base your praise on that particular quality. By doing this, you appear more genuine and will help the narcissist think of a positive perception of you. It will also serve as a constant reminder of the reason you have this person within your circle of friends.

If, for instance, the person who is narcissists is a great writer, make sure you let him know. For instance, you could say, "Yes, you know how to convey your thoughts. I love the way that you manage ideas and communicate them in a clear way." By doing this, that person will be able to see your honesty and is less likely to to harm you.

Chapter 12: Full Blown Narcissistic Partner

A relationship with a narcissistic partner can be very demanding. The traits of a narcissistic partner who are well-developed cannot be changed regardless of the actions you take. The stage could be unnoticed by even the partner being aware about it. He gets a rush of excitement every when he makes his partner feel guilty. He is awed by the tears because they make him feel more powerful and more impressive. When a partner is complaining about him, it's similar to fueling his desires. A narcissistic partner who is fully developed can be identified by the following indicators:

Many factors can lead to dishonesty.

Unhonesty within healthy relationships. Factors such as harassment, fear stress, anxiety and other emotional problems can lead to dishonesty. Narcissists' cases are different. He may betray the relationship since it's part of his personality. He is looking for fulfillment of his desires. He may not be finding the only thing that would satisfy him. So he may betray himself to get out and be a fan of this thing. Narcissists are always lying when in relationships. They'll shift words or make statements which are not true in order that they get the attention of others. If you lie to yourself, you earn the respect of others which is a great achievement for them. Their desire for a high level of appreciation will be satisfied.

Narcissistic partners make promises which they do not keep to win praise. They make promises without worrying for the emotions of their person they are with when they fail to fulfill their promises. They are focused on their current situation and don't think about the next day or even the day after.

Arrogance

The arrogance of others is a sign that someone you love is mature Narcissist. They act in a way which makes you feel inadequate. They don't care about your feelings and if you inquire whether they are interested, they will either decline or respond with rudeness. They'll make important decisions without asking you or even involving you. They could make choices like buying a car, taking huge amounts from joint accounts or filing for divorce and many more.

Their arrogance may extend to guests of the partner or even their friends. Because narcissist partners don't like everything you do and sometimes, they don't like your friends either. Their arrogance may extend to speaking to your friends in as they want, without regard to limits. They'll be like family members and will be rude when you have any inquiries.

The absence of Empathy

A narcissistic, full-time partner is devoid of empathy. The primary concern is his wants. He would like to be praised for the accomplishment of a certain project or to draw attention with an act of faith. He cannot stop his partner from pursuing his desires since he'll be very assertive. The goals of his partner are the main focus. No matter if they put you off your guard in the slightest, or not should not matter to them. He will ensure that his wishes are fulfilled even if it involves a relationship with his spouse. He doesn't think about how his partner will feel after learning about the actions he has taken.

If a partner is sick, the partner will not be able to help. He doesn't consider how much pain his partner is in. All he is concerned about is his own needs. If he needs to eat and his spouse is sick, the are unable to cook. He will lament the inability of his partner to cook. He'll call his partner names. Narcissistic partners cannot experience the pain their partner is going through, regardless of whether he is the one to cause it or not.

Boastful

A person who is narcissistic and has reached the limits of growth has a constant boast. He boasts about how they can make the issue disappear in his relationships. However, at the end of all, they will not have any solutions for the issues. They will brag about how innovative they are in their efforts to get the attention of the public. They will boast about how they have connections to top-of-the-line people to receive exceptional attention and care.

If your partner constantly boasts about how well the relationship is working due to the fact that he is constantly receiving attention. When he brings children to good schools and they boast about, then you must realize that the problem is serious. He's reached the most extreme level of narcissism and the need for help is urgently needed for his recovery.

Envious

It is important to distinguish envy with jealousy. Although jealousy is feelings of regret over the desired thing didn't happen as planned and vice versa, envy is the worst. It's a form of bad thinking. A person who is jealous believes that everything he desires should be the only thing he has and no one else is entitled to it except for himself. Understanding the difference between the two can help you distinguish your partner from a complete Narcissist as well as a growing one.

A partner who is narcissistic has reached their narcissism development peak is an extremely jealous person. He is not willing for him to engage in anything to draw attention. His focus is exclusively on him, and he'll always ensure that he takes the spotlight. He's the kind of person who will envy the latest car of his spouse even when they're together. He'll claim to be happy about the actions of his partner but then trash his partner. He may also tell that the person he is with isn't right so the partner can continue to get it.

Negative Attitude

Negative attitudes towards anything will cause people to leave your company. People do not like people who don't like them or their work. A partner who is narcissistic is at a peak is always negative. He will not support any idea that is proposed by the partner. For instance, if the partner is a great teacher, but has multiple teachers experienced, he'll not be supportive of the profession of teaching. This is due to the fact that the work of his partner is taking the spotlight from him. He believes that he's the only one to be acknowledged or loved.

Selfish

If you're constantly fighting with your partner over not embracing everything your do and his wants and needs are top of mind and he's a Narcissist. He isn't going to change regardless of how much you try. The only thing he requires is mental support by a seasoned psychiatrist. His needs and feelings always come first and he doesn't consider it a problem if his partner has other tasks to complete. He is expecting his partner to take care of all his needs prior to taking care of any other requirements.

A partner who is narcissistic is not able to reciprocate the love extended the them from their loved ones. They are unable to do this because they are selfish enough even in the sense of loving themselves. They think they are not someone worthy of their affection. They fear that they is no way to receive their love back when they give it away Therefore, they keep it for themselves. They are selfish in that they do not think in their mind the emotions of their spouses before they do anything. They strive to be self-important. They're so distracted by their own selfishness and are unable to discern the most important things about the relationship.

The Covert Narcissistic Partner

A covert narcissist can be described as an individual who behaves in a way that can't easily identify. They are incredibly egoistic and want to receives the highest importance. Like any other kind, is not able to feel compassion for others. An undercover narcissist will give you the impression that he is caring however his aim is to have his wants satisfied. He will make it appear that he loves you in order to get back the love. He will congratulate you, purchase gifts for you and other things to accomplish his goals.

Understanding the characteristics of a narcissistic and covert partner can assist you in making the best decision on how to help or end the relationship when his actions are outright violent. They behave in a quiet, in a way that is noticeable and could make you vulnerable before you even realize. These traits provide more information about the hidden narcissistic partner;

Passive Self-importance

In contrast to overtly narcissistic relationships in which their behavior is characterized by aggression and arrogance the introvert partner is more passive. His desire for self-importance is not as obvious and if you're not paying attention, you may not recognize it. You'll only notice the fatigue and fatigue of the behavior after a while. The person who is narcissistic and covertly seeks attention and praise, however, he'll make you feel distinct.

He will try to make it appear as if he's the most beautiful and you'll take a sway to his charms. He will return all the praise you shower him, and then pretend to be in love with you once more. He'll put off completing tasks in order to show you the importance of him to the process. He is enthralled when you tell him that his contribution is unmeasurable. An narcissist in covert mode is a sensitive sense of self-worth, which is why they want you to view him as extraordinary.

Blaming and Shaming

A narcissistic lover who is introverted is gentle with his words. He will gently explain to you what have gone wrong are yours and that you are not the person to be blamed. He will convince you that it's blamed on you, until you begin blame yourself.

You'll be sorry to him for having to suffer through the difficulties that you created. He will make it appear that he's the one who's at fault of this. He is trying to humiliate you by making you look inadequate. He is trying to extract praise from you. He wants to convince that you're worthless. You are not up to his standards and, without him, you'll never be able to achieve it.

In general, he would like you to feel ashamed and to never be anything other than the way he spoke.

The Origin of Confusion

Converting narcissistic partners can ruin your life. They can make you think twice about your choices and they'll influence you to change your views. You'll feel like you've been wrong and you must alter your behavior. Their actions can make them feel better. They would like you to thank them for their efforts and feeling important.

They'll create confusion to create a weak person to allow them to take advantage of you in the way they'd like to. They will make you feel as if they're helping you make answers or make decisions for your issues. In reality, however they're causing confusion. They understand that when you're confused it is impossible to make choices and will view them as essential as they find solutions.

Disregard

The covert type of narcissistic partner is savvy similar to the overt type. In contrast to the obvious type who will manipulate you and reveal the truth to you directly the hidden type of partners will employ other methods. They're not scared of making you look like a failure however their method is distinct and even confusing. For instance, if you have a narcissist who is covertly planning to go out with you and then he's going to stand you up or show up late, without having a reason. He won't give you any reason for the reason he didn't go or the reason he was late.

He has no concern for the relationship, or your needs and time. He thinks he's the more valuable person and is able to do what he pleases anytime. He's a master at ignoring your needs. He causes you to think about so many thoughts. You could convince you that the reason was another way that he could not get to the date.

Emotionally Neglectful

Narcissistic and covert partners can't be a loving couple apart from them. The level of their emotional intelligence can be so poor that they don't even pay attention to how their partners are feeling. They may appear to be nice to you, and perhaps less than polite, but they are emotionally distant. The person who is narcissistic and covert won't praise you for things because they feel that they are elevated and that their self-esteem matters more. He doesn't value your skills or abilities. He will not show the same love and respect you show to him. You'll be in the relationship addressing all emotional issues, and your narcissistic, covertly narcissistic partner doesn't care. But, they appear emotionally connected to you and accessible only when they have an intention of exploitation in order to make you feel embarrassed or insignificant.

Giving with a Purpose

A narcissistic lover who is hidden is not able to reciprocate the love shown towards them by their loved ones. They can't do that because they are selfish to even have love for themselves. They think they are not person worth their affections. They fear that their love will never be returned even if they share it with others Therefore, they keep the love to themselves. They are selfish because they don't keep in mind the thoughts of their loved ones prior to making a decision. They are looking to impress themselves.

Chapter 13: The Differences Between Female And Male Narcissists

Male and female narcissists have the same desire to be the focal point of attention, manipulating others who surround them, and displaying superiority-based beliefs. There are however important differences in the sources they choose to use for their narcissistic sources and the tactics they select to employ among the two genders. The majority of male narcissists are more open, extravagant. They are usually identified more often than women however female narcissists are less sly and evasive in their manipulation and are often described as vulnerable narcissists. If you are aware of the major difference in the ways that the two genders appear and present themselves, you will not be fooled by the less obvious female narcissist that creates fake friends to pull off. Some people who do not comprehend narcissism to believe that she cannot be a narcissist because of her friendship with them. It is also possible to understand the specifics of female and male's different motives, traits and insecurities.

The Female Narcissist

The female narcissist is subdued in her narcissism. She prefers to remain hidden and suck up all attention she gets as required. She is a center of attention and uses her appearance to gain attention. She's often confident and at ease with herself and open about her sexuality. She is not afraid of showing herself as sexually promiscuous and flirty to achieve what she desires. This is why she tends to be obsessed with her appearance, constantly looking perfectly groomed and selecting hairstyles, clothing and makeup that permit her to appear fashionable and classy. Even those not gifted with perfectly symmetrical appearances are confident in their appearance. Many people consider them beautiful romantically as well as platonically. True confidence attracts others because confidence is a sign of confidence. they tend to radiate confidence to others around them too.

Conclusion

If you've ever felt that you are on the verge of becoming dependent, this program is the right program for you. If you've ever felt like you're not capable of breaking this cycle and you are unable to break it, this program is the right program for you. If you are looking to improve the quality of your relationship, this could be for you.

No matter what level you are at or which of these phrases resonates most for you, be aware that this book was designed to help you recognize how to end the cycle that has caused you to lose your self-care and self-love. It will also be looking towards helping you grow more independent in your self-love, how to be a better person and conquer past struggles that still haunt your current.

It is important to realize that kicking the codependency habit isn't something that is easy to accomplish and you'll need to put in the effort to get your life again and get back to full recovery. It's not a fix procedure that can be completed within six weeks. There is no limit to the length of time.

It's a process that will be able to take you from A Z but simultaneously it will educate you and teach you the way to behave from the moment you start. Like all personal journeys there will be bumps and valleys and you may get perplexed by some of the decisions you've made or the anxieties you've developed.

It's all part of the plan, and is important to be embraced in this period of time, in your healing.

If you really desire to end your dependence within the relationship you're in, and you think you are unable to accomplish it on your own I hope this article will help you navigate certain difficult parts. If you are still feeling like you require additional support, you can always talk to friends, relatives or a professional to assist you in whatever way that you require.

Learn all you can find on this topic especially if you've been in a relationship of codependency for a long period of time. Always remember that humans are beings, and our natural tendency is to change as well and one way that you can accomplish this is to get rid of relationships that are toxic and cause harm to yourself.

This book could have (and I hope) led you on a completely different path that you're used to reading and experiencing. I hope you can recover yourself through the power from these phrases.

You now know the truth about codependency. You now know what signs of it are, and how to recognize them so that you can get over these issues. This book will teach how important self-esteem can be as well as the way we think and has taught you ways you can use to boost self-esteem. it has demonstrated that jealousy is an actual emotion and you require strategies similar to those discussed here.

In order to do this, you need to be truthful about yourself and the way you've behaved throughout your life. You must be honest about your awareness and self-awareness and be open to trying something new , which has the potential to alter your life in a radical way for an improved future.

It's not a secret that you'll be unhappy at some point in your journey. At some point, you likely want to end everything in the way it is. It's easier to just complain again and feel the pain from being in a dependency one, since it's easier to confront your personal problems.

Imagine yourself coming to acceptance of who you are, envision the possibilities that you possess Accept change and embrace the new you. Love the person you've finally being, and believe in your desire to be different and achieve the happiness you deserve.

Start today because this is the perfect moment to get your eyes open and realize your current reality. The decision to put things off until later only prolongs how miserable you are and how miserable you feel in the present. I would like to give you valuable insight into the way our minds work and how we can become dependent and the best way to overcome this to be successful throughout our life.

Be confident with the people you would like to spend time with and get comfortable in your thoughts and how you convey your emotions. There is no one else who will help you with this. When you realize the way your mind works and the impact your words can have on your overall wellbeing and well-being, you'll also realize the importance of being able for you to be loved by you and cherish you as the most important person you meet in your life. There is no one more important than you and you are worthy of this joy and love. Don't think about it.

www.ingramcontent.com/pod-product-compliance
Lightning Source LLC
Chambersburg PA
CBHW060330030426
42336CB00011B/1279

* 9 7 8 1 7 7 4 8 5 6 1 5 4 *